Neven Cooks 2

Neven Maguire

Published 2003
Poolbeg Press Ltd.
123 Grange Hill, Baldoyle,
Dublin 13, Ireland
Email: poolbeg@poolbeg.com

1 3 5 7 9 10 8 6 4 2

A catalogue record for this book is available from the British Library.

ISBN 1-84223-130-8

Photography by Kieran Harnett
Designed by Steven Hope
Typeset by Patricia Hope in Trebuchet 9/11

Printed by Nørhaven Book
Viborg, Denmark

www.poolbeg.com

Biography

Neven Maguire has been cooking alongside his mother since he was twelve in their award-winning restaurant in Blacklion, Co Cavan. Although Neven is still in his twenties he has sixteen years of cooking experience behind him and a string of awards to his credit. In 1996, he was 'Eurotoque Young Chef of the Year,' in 1999 and 2000 he was 'Bushmill's Chef of the Year' and in 2001, Neven represented Ireland in the prestigious 'Bocuse d'Or World Cuisine Competition' in France. Neven was a well-kept secret known only to foodies until four years ago when he took up residency in the *Open House* studio as Chef. Now his name is a byword for elegant, classic cooking.

"I am thrilled with this book. I believe it has something in it for everybody, and I do hope you get as much pleasure from it, as I had preparing the food." - Neven Maguire

Acknowledgments

Thanks to everyone at *Open House* and Tyrone Productions. Thanks also to Kieran Harnett for his wonderful photographic talent and the reassuring way he ate everything he photographed! A special mention to John and Georgina for their continued support. I must thank Owen O'Flynn, John and Hugh Martin, Kevin McGovern, Kenneth Moffit, Gerry Galvin and Alastiar McClay, and to all the specialist suppliers who provide me with food which is a delight to work with. A huge thank you must go to Orla Broderick, the brilliant editor of *Neven Cooks 2*. I could not have completed this book without her help. I would also like to specially thank the chefs and entire staff at MacNean Bistro for all their hard work and support throughout this project. Finally, Amelda; thank you for all your help and support, but most of all for always being there.

I would like to dedicate this book to my mother, Vera
and my grandmother, Susan

Contents

Bacon and Black Pudding Salad with Croutons

Serves 4

This salad is my twist on a classic combination, black pudding and apple. Black pudding is such good value for money – buy the best quality you can find; Clonakilty is stocked in most supermarkets or better still get one from a butcher who makes his own. Choose any firm, crisp eating apple and make sure you coat wedges well in all the wonderful buttery juices when turning them under the grill – using a good quality tongs will make this considerably easier.

Ingredients
4oz / 100g white bread, crusts removed (1 day old)
7 tablespoons olive oil
8oz / 225g black pudding, cut into 3/4in / 2cm slices
2 tablespoons apple juice
1 crisp eating apple, peeled, cored and cut into 8 wedges
1oz / 25g butter, at room temperature
icing sugar, to dust
2oz / 50g smoked streaky bacon, cut into small dice
1 tablespoon balsamic vinegar
1 teaspoon wholegrain mustard
1 tablespoon golden syrup
5oz / 150g mixed baby salad leaves
Small handful garlic chive flowers (optional)
salt and freshly ground black pepper

Method Preheat the oven to 180C/350F/Gas 4 and preheat the grill to medium.

To make the croutons, cut or tear the bread into small pieces and then toss the pieces with three tablespoons of the olive oil until they are all well coated. Spread them out on a baking sheet and bake 10-12 minutes until crisp and golden. Remove and leave to cool completely.

Brush the black pudding with the apple juice and arrange on the grill rack with the apple slices. Smear the apple slices with the butter and dust with the icing sugar. Grill to 1-2 minutes on each side until the black pudding is crisp and lightly golden and the apple wedges are caramelised.

Meanwhile, heat a tablespoon of the oil a frying pan, add the diced bacon and fry over a high heat for 3-4 minutes until crisp and golden, stirring. Tip on to some kitchen paper and leave to cool.

To make the dressing, whisk the remaining three tablespoons of the oil with the vinegar, mustard and golden syrup in a small bowl. Season to taste.

To Serve Divide the salad leaves and garlic chive flowers, if using, among serving plates. Scatter over the croutons, black pudding slices, caramelised apple wedges and bacon and then drizzle over the dressing.

Tip If you are not keen on black pudding this salad can also be made with strips of chicken that are pan-fried in a little oil and butter in the same pan as you have used for the bacon.

Mini Pizzas

Serves 4-6

These quick and easy pizzas can be served as an appetizer with drinks; or they are delicious as a starter accompanied by a small green salad. I also really like them drizzled with a sun-dried tomato pesto (page 79), but that of course is an optional extra. Vary the toppings depending on what you have. These ones are great in the spring and summer months.

Ingredients
12 asparagus tips, trimmed
1 small courgette, sliced
1 tablespoon tomato puree
1 tablespoon sweet chilli sauce
1 tablespoon chopped mixed fresh herbs (such as basil and parsley)
2 garlic cloves, finely chopped
5 ripe plum tomatoes, sliced
12 mini white pitta breads
1 small yellow pepper, halved, seeded and sliced
4oz / 100g mozzarella cheese, grated
salt and freshly ground black pepper
lightly dressed green salad (optional)

Method Preheat the oven to 200C/400F/Gas 6.

Blanch the asparagus tips and courgette slices in a pan of boiling salted water for 1-2 minutes until just tender. Drain and quickly refresh. Tip on to kitchen paper and leave to cool.

Place the tomato puree in a small bowl and thin out with a tablespoon of water. Stir in the sweet chilli sauce until well combined. Spread over the pitta breads and sprinkle the herbs and garlic on top.

Cover each of the pitta breads with the tomato slices in a slightly overlapping layer and then scatter over the asparagus tips, courgette and pepper slices. Sprinkle over the mozzarella and arrange on a large baking sheet. Bake for 10-12 minutes or until mozzarella is bubbling and melted.

To Serve Arrange the mini pizzas on warmed serving plates with some salad, if desired.

Tip If mini pitta breads are not available use the normal sized ones and cut them into quarters to serve - you'll need about six in total.

Curried Chicken Spring Rolls with Mango Salsa

Serves 4

This recipe might look like it's got a long list of ingredients, but don't let that put you off. The results are well worth it - I promise. Spring roll wrappers are available in Oriental supermarkets and good delis. Otherwise, consider using thee layers of filo pastry that have been bushed with melted butter before layering up. Bake in a preheated oven 220C/435F/Gas 7 for 10-12 mins

Ingredients

2 boneless skinless chicken breasts
2 teaspoons medium curry powder
2 tablespoons olive oil
1oz / 25g butter
$^1/_2$ head Savoy cabbage, core removed and sliced
4oz / 100g shitake mushroom, stalks trimmed and sliced
1 spring onion, trimmed and finely chopped
2 tablespoons sweet chilli sauce
1 teaspoon chopped fresh coriander
1 tablespoon balsamic vinegar
1 tablespoon light muscovado sugar
dash dark soy sauce
large pinch Chinese five spice powder
$3^1/_2$fl oz / 100ml beef stock
4 spring roll wrappers, thawed if frozen (about 10in / 25cm in diameter)
1 egg, beaten
sunflower oil, for deep-frying

For the Mango Salsa

2 tablespoons finely diced red onion
1 large ripe mango, peeled, stone removed and diced
1 tablespoon fresh lime juice
1 tablespoon sweet chilli sauce
1 tablespoon chopped fresh coriander
salt and freshly ground black pepper

Method Preheat the oven to 190C/375F/Gas 5. To make the filling, place the chicken in a dish and sprinkle over the curry powder and then season generously, tossing to coat. Transfer to a roasting tin, shaking off any excess and drizzle with the olive oil. Roast for 12-15 minutes or until tender and firm to the touch. Remove from the oven and cool. Dice into small cubes and place in a bowl.

Heat the butter in a frying pan and sauté the cabbage and mushrooms for 2-3 minutes until just tender. Season to taste and add to the chicken, reserving the pan. Stir the spring onion into the chicken mixture with the sweet chilli sauce and coriander, mixing to combine. Season to taste and leave to cool.

To make the sauce, return the frying pan to the heat and deglaze with the vinegar, scraping the bottom to remove any sediment. Sprinkle in the sugar, soy sauce, five spice, stirring to combine and then pour in the stock. Simmer for a few minutes until reduced to a sauce consistency. Leave to cool.

Lay one spring roll wrapper on a clean work surface. Brush the edges with a little of the beaten egg. Spoon a quarter of the filling about 3in / 7.5cm away from one of the corners, being careful not to overfill. Roll over to enclose the filling completely, then fold in the two sides and roll up like a cigar. Cover with a dampened clean tea towel and repeat with the remaining ingredients until you have 4 spring rolls.

Heat a deep-fat fryer until 180C/350F or half fill a deep-sided pan with the sunflower oil. Deep-fry the spring rolls for 4-5 minutes until crisp and golden brown. Drain on kitchen paper.

Meanwhile, make the salsa. Tip the red onion into a sieve and pour over enough boiling water to soften. Drain well and tip into a bowl. Add the mango, lime juice, chilli sauce, coriander and season to taste. Set aside for up to 20 minutes to allow the flavours to combine and develop.

To Serve Slice each spring roll into two halves on the diagonal and arrange in the centre of warmed serving plates. Spoon the salsa around the plates and then drizzle with the reserved sauce.

Vegetable Bhajias with Minted Yoghurt Dip

Serves 4-6

These bhajias are delicious just served on their own with the minted yoghurt dip, or try them with a squeeze of lime and/or a selection of your favourite chutneys and pickles. Other vegetables would also work well such as broccoli florets, green beans and courgette or pepper slices, to name but a few.

Ingredients
5oz / 150g gram flour (chickpea flour)
1/2 teaspoon ground cumin seeds
1/2 teaspoon ground coriander seeds
1/4 teaspoon turmeric
1/2 teaspoon garam masala
1 green or red chilli, seeded and finely chopped (optional)
1 teaspoon chopped fresh coriander
sunflower oil, for deep-frying
1 large potato, sliced
1 large onion, sliced
4oz / 100g cauliflower florets
4fl oz / 120ml natural yoghurt
small handful fresh mint leaves
1 spring onion, trimmed and finely chopped
salt and freshly ground black pepper

Method Sift the gram flour into a bowl. Add the spices, chilli (if using) and coriander and then mix well to combine. Season to taste. Make a well in the centre and pour in enough cold water to form a thick batter - you'll need about 3fl oz / 85ml in total. Cover with clingfilm and leave to rest in the fridge for one hour, if time allows.

Heat a deep-fat fryer until 180C/350F or half fill a deep-sided pan with the sunflower oil. Tip all of the vegetables into the batter and mix well to ensure that they are evenly coated. Shake any excess batter from the vegetables and add to the heated oil in small batches. Cook for 3-4 minutes until the vegetables are just tender and the batter is crisp and golden brown. Remove with a slotted spoon and drain on kitchen paper.

To make the minted yoghurt dip, place two tablespoons of the yoghurt in a food processor or liquidiser with the mint, spring onion and whiz until evenly blended. Tip into a bowl and stir in the remaining yoghurt (or you could finely chop the mint and spring onion by hand, it just takes a little more time). Season to taste.

To Serve Pile the vegetable bhajias on to warmed serving plates and add small dishes of the minted yoghurt dip to the side.

Tip These are real bhajias that are made using gram flour (chickpea flour), but you could always improvise and use regular self-raising flour and colour it with half a teaspoon each of ground turmeric and paprika.

Salmon Fish Cakes with Oriental Dipping Sauce

Serves 6-8

These fish cakes would also make an excellent main course for kids who just can't seem to get enough of them. Don't be tempted to over-process the fish cake mixture, as I think it's nice to see chunks of salmon when you cut open a fish cake.

Ingredients
2lb / 900g potatoes, cut into chunks
3oz / 75g carrot, diced
3oz / 75g fresh or frozen peas
1 1/2lb / 750g salmon fillet
3/4 pint / 450ml chicken or vegetable stock
2 tablespoons chopped fresh mixed herbs (such as dill and parsley)
1oz / 25g butter
sunflower oil, for deep-frying
2oz / 50g plain flour
2 eggs, beaten
5oz / 150g fresh white breadcrumbs
1 tablespoon sesame seeds

For the Oriental Dipping Sauce
6 tablespoons dark soy sauce
3 tablespoons clear honey
1 teaspoon light muscovado sugar
1 teaspoon toasted sesame oil
1 red birds eye chilli, seeded and thinly sliced
1 teaspoon finely grated fresh root ginger
1 small lemon grass stalk, outer leaves removed and finely chopped
salt and freshly ground black pepper
lime wedges, to garnish

Method To make the dipping sauce, place the soy sauce in a small pan with the honey, sugar, sesame oil, chilli, ginger and lemon grass. Place over a gentle heat and infuse for 5 minutes, stirring occasionally. Remove from the heat and leave for 20 minutes to allow the flavours to develop. Then strain into a sterilised jar or bottle.

Cook the potatoes in a covered pan of boiling salted water for 15-20 minutes until tender. Drain and then mash until smooth. Leave to cool slightly. Place the carrots in a pan of boiling salted water and bring to a simmer, then cook for 2 minutes. Add the peas and cook for another 2-3 minutes until tender. Drain and quickly refresh.

Place the salmon in a sauté pan with a lid and pour in the stock to cover. Cover the pan and bring to a simmer, then poach for 5-7 minutes until the salmon is just tender. Remove from the heat and leave to cool in the liquid.

Transfer the cooled salmon to a plate and flake the flesh, discarding any skin and bones. Tip into a bowl and add the mashed potatoes, herbs, carrots and peas. Melt the butter in a small pan or in the microwave and add to the salmon mix, mixing to combine and season to taste. Shape into 16 patties, each about 3in /7.5cm in diameter and 1in / 2.5cm thick. Cover with clingfilm and chill for at least 20 minutes (or up to 24 hours is fine) to firm up.

Heat a deep-fat fryer until 180C/350F or half fill a deep-sided pan with the sunflower oil. Tip the flour on to a plate and season generously. Place the eggs in a shallow dish and the breadcrumbs in another dish with the sesame seeds, mixing to combine. Dust the chilled patties in the seasoned flour, shaking off any excess. Dip in the beaten egg, turning to coat and then cover with the sesame breadcrumbs. Deep-fry the fish cakes for 4-5 minutes until heated through and golden brown. You may have to do this in batches. Drain on kitchen paper.

To Serve Arrange the salmon fish cakes on serving plates with lime wedges and place small dishes of the Oriental dipping sauce to the side.

Tip For a healthier option, cook the fish cakes in a large frying pan with a knob of butter and a little oil for about 5 minutes on each side until crisp and golden.

Feta Cheese and Red Onion Frittata

Serves 4-6

This is one of my favourite frittatas. The sweetness of the red onion and leek complements the saltiness of the feta cheese perfectly. It is good served hot or cold and makes an excellent vegetarian option. Alternatively, cut into small wedges and serve as part of antipasti platter with Parma ham, roasted peppers and semi sun-dried tomatoes. It also makes great picnic food as it is so easy to transport – the possibilities are endless!

Ingredients
1oz / 25g butter
1 tablespoon olive oil
1 red onion, sliced
1 leek, trimmed and thinly sliced
(about 5oz / 150g in total)
8 eggs, beaten
4oz / 100g feta cheese, crumbled
1 tablespoon torn fresh basil
1 tablespoon freshly grated Parmesan
salt and freshly ground black pepper
lightly dressed herb salad, to serve (optional)

Method Preheat the oven to 180C/350F/Gas 4.

Heat an ovenproof frying pan that is about 9in / 23cm in diameter over a medium heat. Add the butter and olive oil and then tip in the red onion and leeks. Sauté for about 5 minutes until softened but not coloured.

Season the eggs and gently stir into the vegetable mixture and cook for 2 minutes over a low heat to set the bottom and the sides. Sprinkle over the crumbled feta cheese, basil and Parmesan and cook gently for another 5 minutes until the bottom and sides are well set and lightly golden. Transfer to the oven and cook, uncovered for 15-20 minutes until just set, puffed up and lightly golden.

To Serve Loosen the sides of the frittata with a palette knife, turn out on to a large plate and cut into wedges. Serve warm or cold on serving plates with the herb salad, if desired.

Tip This frittata can be cooked completely on the hob over a very gentle heat and then just flashed under a grill for about 5 minutes to finish cooking. You'll just need to be very careful that the bottom doesn't catch and burn.

Roasted Red Pepper Gazpacho with Basil Oil

Serves 4

This is a very simple recipe that's great to make when there are plenty of superbly flavoured tomatoes to hand. It is just so deliciously light and fresh, making it perfect to serve on a warm summer's day. However, it is worth remembering that as it is served well chilled it will need to be highly seasoned to bring out the best flavour.

Ingredients
2 large red peppers
1lb / 450g very ripe vine tomatoes, roughly chopped
1 garlic clove, chopped
2 tablespoons tomato puree
1 tablespoon finely chopped onion
handful fresh basil leaves, plus extra to garnish
1 pint / 600ml vegetable stock, chilled
1 small ciabatta loaf, cut into cubes (about 6in / 15cm in diameter)
2 tablespoons olive oil
1 tablespoon freshly grated Parmesan

For the Basil Oil
bunch fresh basil (stalks removed)
1/4 pint / 150ml olive oil
salt and freshly ground black pepper

Method Preheat the oven to 220C/425F/Gas 7.
Place the peppers on a baking sheet and roast for 20-25 minutes or until the skins are black and blistered, and the flesh has softened. Once they are cool enough to handle, peel away the skin and discard with the stalks and seeds. Then chop up the flesh.

Place the roasted red pepper flesh in a food processor or a liquidiser with the tomatoes, garlic, tomato puree, onion and the basil leaves. Blend for a minute or so until smooth, then with the motor still running, slowly add the stock until well combined. Pour into a jug and season to taste. Cover with clingfilm and chill for at least 2 hours (or overnight is fine) to allow the flavours to develop.

Reduce the oven temperature to 190C/375F/Gas 5. Toss the ciabatta cubes in a bowl with the olive oil and Parmesan until evenly coated. Tip on to a baking sheet and cook for 10-12 minutes until crisp and golden. Leave on the baking sheet until completely cool, then store in an airtight container if not using immediately.

To make the basil oil, place the basil leaves in a mini processor or liquidiser with the olive oil and blend until smooth. Pass the speckled oil through a fine sieve set over a jug and then transfer to a plastic squeezy bottle or screw-topped jar. Chill until ready to use.

To Serve Ladle the gazpacho into chilled serving bowls and add a swirl of the basil oil. Garnish with the croutons and some torn basil leaves.

Tip If you like a really smooth finish, pass the soup through a sieve set over a large jug or bowl, using the back of a ladle to help press it through.

French Onion Soup

Serves 4-6

This classic French bistro soup is my Mum's favourite so I often find myself making a batch. It really is a soup that people never seem to tire off and it always sells well in the restaurant. If you have heatproof serving bowls, fill with the piping hot soup and float the toasted baguette slices on top. Sprinkle over the Gruyère and then grill until the cheese is bubbling and melted.

Ingredients
2oz / 50g butter
1 1/2lb / 675g onions, thinly sliced
1 tablespoon sugar
1oz / 25g plain flour
1 3/4 pints / 1 litre brown chicken or beef stock
1 tablespoon cider vinegar
1 small baguette, cut into slices
2oz / 50g Gruyère cheese, finely grated
2 teaspoons chopped fresh parsley
salt and freshly ground black pepper

Method Melt the butter in a large pan and add the onions and sugar. Cook the onions over a very low heat for about 15 minutes until well softened and golden brown, stirring occasionally so the onions do not stick as they caramelise.

Stir the flour into the onion mixture and cook over a very low heat for another 5 minutes, stirring continuously. Gradually pour in the stock and add the vinegar, stirring to prevent any lumps forming. Bring to the boil, then reduce the heat and simmer for 15-20 minutes until the onions are meltingly tender and the soup has thickened, stirring occasionally. Season to taste.

Preheat the grill to high. Arrange the baguette slices on the grill rack and toast on both sides. Sprinkle the Gruyère and parsley on top and cook for another 1-2 minutes until bubbling and melted.

To Serve Ladle the soup into warmed serving bowls and arrange the Gruyère toasts on top.

Tip Use any type of Swiss cheese that is available or try an equal mixture of Gruyère and Parmesan, which works equally well.

Leek and Potato Soup with Smoked Bacon

Serves 4-6

My Mum used to make this all the time when we were young. We'd get a big bowl as soon as we got in from school on a cold winter's evening to keep us going until our dinner. It can also be served chilled, but I prefer it piping hot and served with a chunk of homemade bread.

Ingredients

2oz / 50g butter
1lb / 450g leeks, trimmed and roughly chopped
8 rindless smoked streaky bacon rashers
1 onion, roughly chopped (about 8oz / 225g in total)
1 potato, cut into cubes (about 8oz / 225g in total)
1oz / 25g plain flour
3 pints / 1.75 litres chicken stock
7fl oz / 200ml cream
12 fresh basil leaves, plus extra to garnish
salt and freshly ground black pepper

Method Preheat the grill to medium.

Cut four of the bacon rashers in half again and arrange on the grill rack. Cook for 3-4 minutes on each side until crisp and golden. Transfer to a plate and set aside to use as a garnish. Dice the remaining four rashers.

Melt the butter in a large pan and gently fry the diced bacon with the leeks and onion over a low heat for about 5 minutes until softened but not coloured. Add the potato and flour, stirring well to combine and then cook for another 2 minutes, stirring. Gradually add the stock, stirring to prevent any lumps forming. Bring to the boil, then reduce the heat and simmer for 15 minutes or until the potatoes are completely tender, stirring occasionally.

Add 1/4 pint / 150ml of the cream to the soup and simmer for another 5 minutes, stirring occasionally. Add the basil and season to taste. Remove from the heat and reserve a large spoonful of potatoes cubes to use as a garnish. Puree the soup in batches in a food processor or liquidiser until smooth, then pour back into a clean pan; or use a hand-held blender leaving the soup in the pan. Season to taste and reheat gently. Place the remaining 2fl oz / 50ml of cream in a bowl and lightly whip.

To Serve Divide the reserved hot potato cubes between warmed serving bowls. Ladle over the soup and drizzle the whipped cream on top. Garnish with the crispy bacon rashers and some basil leaves to serve.

Tip I reserve some of the cooked potato cubes to give the finished soup texture, but if you decide to prepare it in advance these will need to be reheated in the microwave or in a small pan with a tiny knob of butter to prevent them from sticking until heated through.

Carrot and Parsnip Soup with Nutmeg Cream

Serves 4-6

This has to be one of the easiest and most versatile soups I know. It has a wonderful warm autumnal colour and is literally ready in minutes. Just be careful not to add too much nutmeg to the whipped cream as it is a very powerful spice and should only ever be used sparingly.

Ingredients
8oz / 225g carrots, cut into chunks
8oz / 225g parsnips, cut into chunks
1 small onion, cut into chunks
1oz / 25g butter
2 pints / 1.2 litres chicken stock
1oz / 25g plain flour
3fl oz / 85ml cream
good pinch fresh grated nutmeg
2 teaspoons chopped fresh parsley, plus extra to garnish
salt and freshly ground black pepper

Method Place the carrots, parsnips and onion in a food processor and pulse until finely chopped, but be careful not to overdo it as you want to keep some texture (or you can do this by hand, it just takes a bit longer).

Heat the butter in a large heavy-based pan. Add the vegetables and cook gently for 5 minutes or until softened but not coloured, stirring occasionally. Stir in the flour and cook over a low heat for another 5 minutes, stirring continuously.

Heat the stock in a separate pan until simmering, then gradually add to the vegetable and flour mixture, stirring constantly to prevent any lumps forming. Bring to the boil, then reduce the heat and stir in 2fl oz / 50ml of the cream and the parsley and then allow to just heat through. Season to taste.

Place the remaining 1fl oz / 25ml of cream in a bowl and lightly whip, then fold in the nutmeg.

To Serve Ladle the soup into warmed serving bowls and add a dollop of the nutmeg cream. Garnish with the parsley.

Tip The vegetables can be varied; experiment with sweet potatoes or butternut squash or even celeriac works well.

Wild Mushroom and Parsley Soup

Serves 4-6

Soup made from wild mushrooms has the most extraordinary, intense flavour. There is now a decent range available from supermarkets and good greengrocers, depending on the time of year. Look out for chanterelle, shitake, oyster, morels and horn of plenty, or mixed packet selections. Although there are many edible mushrooms growing in the wild, I suggest unless you know what you are doing that you leave them well alone. In France you are able to take wild mushrooms to the pharmacy to be checked and identified. Imagine trying to do that here . . . you'd probably be locked up!

Ingredients
6oz / 175g wild mushrooms, cleaned
6oz / 175g button mushrooms
1 small onion, chopped
9oz / 250g potatoes, roughly chopped
1oz / 25g butter
2 tablespoons olive oil
1 garlic clove, crushed
4fl oz / 120ml white wine
2 pints / 1.2 litres chicken stock
4-6 tablespoons soured cream
salt and freshly ground black pepper
fresh parsley sprigs, to garnish

Method Place all the mushrooms and the onion in a food processor and pulse until finely chopped (or you can do this by hand, it just takes a bit longer). Tip into a bowl and repeat the process with the potatoes.

Heat the butter and oil in a large pan over a medium heat. Add the mushroom and onion mixture with the garlic and cook for 10 minutes, stirring occasionally. Stir in the potatoes and then pour in the wine and stock. Bring to the boil, then reduce the heat and simmer for 20 minutes or until the potatoes are completely tender and the liquid has slightly reduced.

Puree the soup in batches in a food processor or liquidiser until smooth, then pour back into a clean pan, or use a hand-held blender leaving the soup in the pan. Season to taste and reheat gently.

To Serve Ladle the soup into warmed serving bowls and drizzle a tablespoon of soured cream into each one. Garnish with the parsley sprigs.

Tip This soup is perfect to use mushrooms that are slightly past their best. They really do make the best soup when they are a few days old and have darkened a bit.

Fragrant Prawn and Coconut Soup

Serves 4

Coconut milk is one of my favourite ingredients. It makes a fantastic creamy base for all the other robust flavours in this Asian-inspired soup. Thai fish sauce (nam pla) is a fermented sauce that is used in Thai cooking as a seasoning. There really is no substitute so just season with salt and pepper if you don't want to use it.

Ingredients
2 potatoes, cut into dice
1 tablespoon vegetable oil
1 onion, thinly sliced
1 garlic clove, crushed
1 teaspoon freshly grated root ginger
1 tablespoon Thai red curry paste
4 teaspoons tomato puree
1/2 pint / 300ml vegetable stock
1 tablespoon Thai fish sauce (nam pla)
14oz / 400g can coconut milk
6oz / 175g fine green beans, trimmed and halved
8oz / 225g raw tiger prawns, peeled and cleaned (with tails left on)
2 tablespoons natural yoghurt
2 spring onions, trimmed and finely sliced (optional)
2oz / 50g desiccated or toasted coconut flakes
fresh coriander sprigs, to garnish

Method Cook the potatoes in a pan of boiling salted water for 10 minutes or until just tender and holding their shape, then drain.

Meanwhile, heat the oil in a pan and gently fry the onion, garlic and ginger for 5 minutes until softened but not coloured, stirring occasionally. Stir in the Thai curry paste and cook for 1 minute, stirring.

Add the tomato puree to the pan with the vegetable stock, Thai fish sauce and coconut milk. Bring to the boil, then reduce the heat and simmer for 10 minutes until slightly reduced, stirring occasionally. Stir the green beans, prawns and cooked potato dice and simmer for another 2 minutes or until the beans are tender and the prawns are cooked through.

To Serve Ladle the soup into the warmed serving bowls. Add a swirl of the yoghurt and scatter over the spring onions if using and toasted coconut flakes. Garnish with the coriander sprigs.

Tip Thai red curry paste is now available in jars from all large supermarkets, but very good quality ones can be found in Oriental supermarkets. It will keep for a relatively decent time if stored in the fridge once opened. I normally keep mine topped up with a thin layer of oil to ensure the flavours stay fresh.

MERMAID

Braised Lamb Shanks with Barley and Rosemary

Serves 6

This is wonderful for cold days and perfect for serving when you want to relax and enjoy the company with no last minute hurdles. When buying the lamb shanks, ask your butcher to trim off any excess fat and remove the knuckles - it will save what can be a difficult job. They are extremely good value for money. It's well worth seeking them out.

Ingredients

1 tablespoon vegetable oil
6 lamb shanks, well trimmed and knuckles removed
7oz / 200g carrots, cut into wedges
1 onion, roughly chopped
4 garlic cloves, peeled
1 fresh thyme sprig
1 fresh rosemary sprig, plus extra to garnish
2oz / 50g pearl barley, washed
3 ½ pints / 2 litres beef stock
1 pint / 600ml red wine
1 teaspoon light muscovado sugar (optional)
12 baby pearl onions, peeled
2 ¼lb / 1kg potatoes, cut into chunks
3oz / 75g butter
1 bunch spring onions, trimmed and finely chopped (about 6 in total)
salt and freshly ground black pepper

Method Preheat the oven to 160C/325F/Gas 3.
Heat oil in a large casserole with a lid over a high heat. Add the lamb shanks and fry until lightly browned on all sides, turning regularly with a tongs. Transfer to a plate and set aside. Add the carrots, onion and garlic to the pan and sauté for about 5 minutes until lightly golden. Tip into a bowl and set aside.

Return the lamb shanks to the casserole with the herbs and barley. Pour over the stock and wine to cover. Season to taste and cover tightly with foil and then the lid. Bake for 1½ hours. Remove the casserole from the oven, add the reserved vegetables and pearl onions and cook for another hour until the lamb is very tender and almost falling off the bone.

Strain the cooking liquid into a separate pan and then put the lid back on the casserole to keep the lamb shanks and vegetables warm. Bring the cooking liquid back to a simmer, then cook until reduced to a sauce consistency. Season to taste and if you think that the sauce is too bitter add the sugar.

Meanwhile, cook the potatoes in a pan of boiling salted water for 15-20 minutes or until completely tender. Drain and mash until smooth. Melt the butter in a sauté pan over a medium heat and sauté the spring onions for 2-3 minutes until tender but not coloured. Beat in the mashed potatoes and season to taste.

To Serve Spoon the mashed potatoes on to serving plates and arrange a lamb shank on top of each one. Spoon the vegetables to the side and drizzle around the reduced sauce. Garnish with rosemary sprigs.

Tip The flavour of this dish only improves if you make it a day ahead - just reheat gently on top of the stove to serve.

Chilli Lamb Kebabs with Lemon Cous Cous

Serves 4

You can buy chilli oil in large supermarkets or good delis, but it is really easy to make it yourself. Simply heat 3/4 pint / 450ml of olive oil gently with three dried red chillies for about 5 minutes to allow the flavours to infuse. Leave until completely cool and then transfer to a clean screw-topped jar or bottle, label and use within two months of opening. I always have a bottle to hand and use it all the time in stir fries and marinades.

Ingredients
1 mild red chilli, seeded and finely chopped
1 tablespoon clear honey
2 tbsp dark soy sauce
2 garlic cloves, crushed
1 teaspoon finely chopped fresh root ginger
1 teaspoon chilli oil
2 1/4lb / 1kg lamb neck fillets, well trimmed and cut into 1in / 2.5cm cubes
1/4 pint / 150ml natural yoghurt
3in / 7.5cm piece cucumber, seeds removed and finely grated
2 tablespoons chopped fresh parsley, plus extra springs to garnish

For the Cous Cous
12fl oz / 350ml vegetable stock
8oz / 225g cous cous
1 tablespoon olive oil
1 small red onion, finely chopped
1 garlic clove, finely chopped
finely grated rind of 1 lemon
1 tablespoon chopped fresh coriander
salt and freshly ground black pepper

Method Place the chilli in a shallow non-metallic dish with the honey, soy sauce, garlic, ginger and chilli oil and then mix well to combine. Add the lamb, stirring to coat, and then cover with clingfilm and chill for 2 hours to marinade (or up to 24 hours is fine if time allows).

Heat a griddle or heavy-based frying pan over a medium heat. Thread the marinated lamb on to 8 x 8in / 20cm metal or bamboo skewers. Cook on the heated pan over for 12-15 minutes, turning frequently until cooked through and lightly charred - you'll probably have to do this in batches. Season to taste.

To make the cous cous, place the stock in a pan and bring to a simmer. Tip the cous cous into a heatproof bowl and pour over the hot stock. Set aside for 15 minutes to allow the grains to swell.

Meanwhile, heat the olive oil in a frying pan and sauté the onion, garlic and lemon rind for 2-3 minutes until softened but not coloured. Fluff up the cous cous with a fork and then fold in the onion mixture with the coriander. Season to taste. The cous cous can be used immediately or left to cool, covered with clingfilm and chilled until needed. Reheat in the microwave or in the bottom of a low oven covered loosely with foil.

To make the cucumber raita, place the yoghurt in a serving bowl and stir in the cucumber and parsley. Season to taste and mix well to combine. Cover with clingfilm and chill until needed. This can be made up to 24 hours in advance.

To Serve Spoon the cous cous into centre of warmed serving plates and arrange two kebabs on top of each one. Add a good dollop of the cucumber raita to the side and garnish with the parsley sprigs.

Tip These kebabs would also cook brilliantly on the barbecue and then served stuffed into warm pitta breads with plenty of salad before being drizzled with the raita to serve.

Pork and Mushroom Stroganoff

Serves 4

Forget what you've been told about pork being fatty and unhealthy; it can be very lean, as in this dish, so it just about makes up for all the cream I've used! I like to serve this stroganoff with the tagliatelle which is traditional, but it could be equally delicious with my roasted garlic mash (page 35) or cooked basmati rice. (page 71)

Ingredients
7oz / 200g tagliatelle
1 tablespoon plain flour
2 teaspoon paprika
1lb / 450g pork fillet, trimmed and sliced
2 tablespoons vegetable oil
1oz / 25g butter
1 onion, sliced
8oz / 225g button mushrooms, halved
1 garlic clove, crushed
4 tablespoons white wine
1/4 pint / 150ml chicken stock
1 teaspoon Dijon mustard
2 teaspoons tomato puree
1/4 pint / 150ml cream
2 tablespoons chopped fresh parsley
salt and freshly ground black pepper

Method Cook the tagliatelle in a large pan of boiling salted water for 8-10 minutes until 'al dente' or according to packet instructions. Sprinkle the flour and paprika on a flat plate and season generously. Add the pork slices and then toss until evenly coated, shaking off any excess.

Heat a large pan over a high heat. Add half the oil and butter and once sizzling, tip in the dusted pork. Sauté for 5 minutes until golden, then transfer to a plate with a slotted spoon and set aside.

Add the remaining oil and butter to the pan and then add the onion, mushrooms and garlic. Sauté for 5 minutes until tender. Return pork to pan and stir well to combine. Add the wine, stock, mustard and tomato puree and cook for about 5 minutes until slightly reduced, stirring occasionally. Stir in the cream, bring to the boil, then reduce the heat and simmer gently for a couple of minutes and cook until sauce has thickened and slightly reduced. Season to taste.

To Serve Drain the pasta and divide among warmed serving plates. Make a slight well in the centre of each serving and spoon over the stroganoff. Garnish with the parsley.

Tip Boneless, skinless chicken thighs are very succulent and would work perfectly instead of the pork in this recipe.

Roast Pork with Apricot and Pine Nut Stuffing

Serves 6-8

For good crackling, look for a joint of pork that has a thick, dry layer of skin - organic is always best and quite good value for money considering the price of some of the other meats. If possible, allow the skin to dry out for a day uncovered and skin-side up on a large plate in the fridge.

Ingredients
75g / 3oz butter
1 onion, finely chopped
1 garlic clove, crushed
2oz / 50g pine nuts
175g / 6oz fresh white breadcrumbs (day-old)
2oz / 50g ready-to-eat dried apricots, roughly chopped
1 tablespoon roughly chopped fresh parsley
1 teaspoon fresh thyme leaves
4lb / 1.75kg boneless pork loin, skin scored at 1/4in / 0.5mm intervals
2 tablespoons olive oil

For the Gravy
1 tablespoon plain flour
3 tablespoons ruby red port or red wine
1 tablespoon clear honey
4 whole cloves
1 pint / 600ml beef stock
sea salt and freshly ground black pepper
roast potatoes (page 113) and a selection of vegetables, to serve

Method Preheat oven to 200C/400F/Gas 6. Melt the butter in a pan and gently fry the onion and garlic for 3-4 minutes until softened but not coloured, stirring occasionally. Heat a frying pan and toast the pine nuts, tossing to ensure they colour evenly. Stir the breadcrumbs into the onion mixture with the apricots, parsley and thyme. Stir in the toasted pine nuts and season. Remove from the heat to cool.

Place the pork joint skin-side down, on a board and trim down to give a good shape. Spoon the cooled stuffing along the centre, roll up the joint and tie with string at 1in / 2.5cm intervals to secure.

Transfer the stuffed pork joint to a large roasting tin and pat the skin dry with kitchen paper and then rub the olive oil into the skin with plenty of sea salt. Cover with foil and roast for 20 minutes. Reduce the heat to 180C/350F/Gas 4 and roast for another 15 minutes and then remove the foil and cook for another 1 1/4 hours or until the pork is tender and the crackling is crisp and golden.

When the pork is cooked, transfer to a warmed serving plate and leave it to rest for about 15 minutes. Meanwhile, make the gravy. Pour off most of the fat from the roasting tin and place on the hob over a gentle heat. Stir in the flour and cook for 2 minutes, stirring. Slowly pour in the port or wine and then add the honey and cloves, stirring to combine. Gradually add the stock, stirring continuously. Bring to the boil, then reduce the heat and simmer for 10 minutes until reduced and thickened, stirring occasionally. Season to taste.

Cut the string from the rested pork joint and cut through the fat just underneath the crackling. Remove and cut into pieces and then carve the pork into thick slices.

To Serve Arrange the pork slices on warmed serving plates and serve with the roast potatoes, gravy and vegetables of your choice.

Tip Do not be tempted to baste the rind during cooking and if the rind still hasn't crackled by the time the joint is cooked, remove and snip into strips with a scissors, then place under the grill until done.

Steak and Onion Open Sandwich

Serves 2

There are times when you want something tasty and delicious but just don't feel like cooking a full meal. This is one of those dishes that I find myself cooking again and again. If you want to make it even more substantial try serving it with crisp, fat chips and watch how quickly the plates are cleared!

Ingredients
3 tablespoons olive oil
2 large red onions, sliced and separated cut into rings
1 tablespoon light muscovado sugar
1 tablespoon balsamic vinegar
2 x 6oz / 175g thin cut rump or sirloin steak
4 tablespoons mayonnaise (homemade or from a jar is fine)
1 teaspoon Dijon mustard
1 teaspoon wholegrain mustard
2 ripe tomatoes, sliced
2oz / 50g wild rocket
1 small ciabatta loaf (about 6in / 15cm in diameter)
salt and freshly ground black pepper

Method Heat two tablespoons of the oil in a large frying pan and preheat the grill. Fry onions for 10 minutes until softened and golden, stirring occasionally. Sprinkle over the sugar and balsamic vinegar and then cook for another 2 minutes until the sugar has dissolved and is slightly syrupy, stirring continuously. Tip into a bowl and keep warm.

Return the pan to the heat and add the remaining tablespoon of oil. Season the steaks, add them to the pan and cook over a high heat for 3-4 minutes on each side for well done; or according to taste.

Split the ciabatta in half and then arrange on the grill rack cut-side up. Place under the grill until lightly toasted. Mix the mayonnaise in a small bowl with the two mustards.

To Serve Place a piece of the toasted ciabatta on each warmed serving plate. Add a smear of the mustard mayonnaise and then arrange a layer of the tomato slices. Season to taste and add the rocket. Place the steak on top and add the reserved fried onions. Drizzle over the mustard mayonnaise (see tip).

Tip I normally make up a larger batch of the mustard mayonnaise and then store it in a squeezy plastic bottle (just like the one you get in restaurants with tomato ketchup) in the fridge. This will also help you achieve the clever criss-cross drizzle lines that chefs tend to do for presentation.

Sirlion Steak Diane with Roasted Garlic Mash

Serves 4

As with fashion, food trends come and go, but this is one recipe that has stood the test of time. I've got my Mum to thank for it and once you have had a bite I have no doubt you'll realise why. The roasted garlic mash makes the perfect accompaniment to soak up the rich, creamy sauce.

Ingredients
2 tablespoons olive oil
1oz / 25g butter
1 shallot, finely chopped
5oz / 150g button mushrooms, sliced
4fl oz / 120ml brandy
$^1/_4$ pint / 150ml white wine
$^1/_4$ pint / 150ml beef stock
2 tablespoons Worcestershire sauce
good pinch sugar
$^1/_4$ pint / 150ml cream
1 tablespoon chopped fresh parsley
squeeze of fresh lemon juice
4 x 8oz / 225g sirloin steaks

For the Roasted Garlic Mash
4 garlic cloves (unpeeled)
1 tablespoon olive oil
$1^1/_2$lb / 675g potatoes, cut into chunks
1oz / 25g butter
1 tablespoon cream
salt and freshly ground black pepper
fresh chervil sprigs, to garnish (optional)

Method Preheat the oven to 180C/350F/Gas 4. To make the roasted garlic for the mash, place the garlic on a square of foil and drizzle over the olive oil. Scrunch up the foil into a purse, place on a baking sheet and roast for 30 minutes until completely tender. Remove the foil parcel from the oven, open out and set aside to cool.

To make the sauce, heat a pan and add one of the tablespoons of the oil and the butter, then swirl until the butter has melted and is foaming. Tip in the shallot and mushrooms and sauté for 2-3 minutes until tender. Sprinkle over the brandy. It will flame up for about 5-10 seconds and then subside when the alcohol flame burns off. Add white wine and simmer until reduced by half.

Stir the stock into the pan with the Worcestershire sauce, sugar and cream. Bring to the boil, then reduce the heat and simmer for 10-15 minutes or until reduced to a sauce consistency, stirring occasionally. Stir in the parsley and lemon juice. Season to taste and then set aside and keep warm until ready to serve.

To make the mash, cook the potatoes in a pan of boiling salted water for 15-20 minutes until tender. Drain and mash until smooth. Melt the butter in a frying pan with the cream and squeeze in the flesh from the garlic, mashing with a fork. Beat into the potatoes and season. Spoon into a piping bag with a 1in / 2.5cm nozzle.

Meanwhile, season the steaks with pepper. Heat the remaining oil in a large ovenproof frying pan until smoking hot. Add the steaks, making sure not to overcrowd the pan. Sear for 2 minutes on each side to seal in the juices. Transfer to the oven and cook for another 5 minutes if you like your steaks rare or 7 minutes if you prefer them medium, or 10 minutes for well done. When the steaks are cooked, leave them to rest in a warm place for about 5 minutes and stir any juices that run off the steaks into the reserved sauce.

To Serve Arrange the steak on the side of warmed serving plates and spoon over the sauce. Pipe some garlic mash beside each one and garnish with the chervil sprigs.

Tip Rib eye steaks are a good alternative as they are extremely good value for money.

Spaghetti Bolognaise

Serves 6-8

Ask people what their speciality is in the kitchen and Spaghetti Bolognaise is often the answer. Well this recipe is the real McCoy and definitely doesn't use any of those readymade pasta sauces. It's is a perfect stand-by for converting into dishes such as moussaka, cannelloni, chilli con carne, lasagne, cottage pie and as a filling for pancakes and jacket potatoes . . . need I go on. It's just so versatile that it is worth the two hours cooking time. This is to allow the meat to break down and come completely soft and tender – trust me it's worth it!

Ingredients

1 tablespoon olive oil
1oz / 25g butter
1 onion, finely chopped
2 carrots, finely chopped
2 celery sticks, finely chopped
2 garlic cloves, crushed
8oz / 225g button mushrooms, sliced
4oz / 100g rindless smoked streaky bacon, finely chopped
12oz / 350g lean minced beef
1 tablespoon tomato puree
¼ pint / 150ml dry white wine
2 x 14oz / 400g cans chopped tomatoes
½ pint / 300ml beef stock
1 tablespoon cream
1 tablespoon chopped fresh basil
1½lb / 675g spaghetti
6-8 tablespoons freshly grated Parmesan
salt and freshly ground black pepper
warm Italian crusty bread, to serve

Method Heat the butter and oil in a large sauté pan with a lid until sizzling. Add the onion, carrots, celery, garlic, mushrooms and bacon and sauté over a medium heat for 10 minutes until the vegetables have softened and everything is lightly browned, stirring frequently.

Add the minced beef to the pan, reduce the heat and cook gently for 10 minutes until well browned, stirring to break up any lumps with a wooden spoon. Stir in the wine and simmer for 5 minutes until reduced. Stir in the tomato puree, canned tomatoes and half of the stock and bring to the boil, stirring to combine.

Reduce the heat under the pan, half cover with the lid and simmer very gently for about 2 hours or until the meat is meltingly tender, stirring occasionally and adding a little more of the remaining stock as it becomes absorbed.

Add the cream and basil to the sauce and mix well to combine, then simmer uncovered for another 30 minutes until the bolognaise sauce is well reduced and thickened, stirring frequently. Season to taste.

Meanwhile, cook the spaghetti in a large pan of boiling salted water for 8-10 minutes until 'al dente' or according to packet instructions.

To Serve Drain the cooked spaghetti and tip into a large warmed serving bowl. Ladle over the bolognaise sauce and toss well to combine. Transfer to warm individual serving bowls and sprinkle over the Parmesan. Have a separate basket of the crusty bread to hand around.

Tip I often make double the quantity of the bolognaise sauce and then freeze it in small batches.

Sizzling Beef Fajitas with Guacamole and Tomato Salsa

Serves 4

Kids just seem to love this dish and luckily it's actually very good for them and full of protein. I always keep a packet of flour tortillas in the cupboard as they often come in handy.

Ingredients

3 tablespoons vegetable oil
1 large onion, thinly sliced
1 red, 1 green and 1 yellow pepper, seeded and cut into thin strips
1¹/4lb / 550g frying steak, trimmed and sliced into strips (good quality)
1oz / 25g fajita seasoning mix
2 limes
8 soft flour tortillas (1 packet)
¹/4 pint / 150ml soured cream
1 bunch spring onions, trimmed and thinly sliced (about 6 in total)

For the Tomato Salsa

1 tablespoon olive oil
1 small onion, roughly chopped
1 garlic clove, crushed
14oz / 400g can chopped tomatoes
2oz / 50g jalapeño peppers, finely chopped (from a jar - optional)
¹/4 teaspoon sugar
pinch hot chilli powder
3 tablespoons roughly chopped fresh coriander

For the Guacamole

2 ripe avocados
1 small red onion, finely chopped
1 garlic clove, crushed
1 red chilli, seeded and finely chopped
2 tomatoes, peeled, seeded and roughly chopped
2 tablespoons roughly chopped fresh coriander
finely grated rind and juice of 1 lime
salt and freshly ground black pepper

Method To make the salsa, heat the oil in a pan and gently fry the onion and garlic for 3-4 minutes until softened but not coloured, stirring occasionally. Add the canned tomatoes, jalapeños peppers, if using, sugar and chilli powder. Bring to a simmer and then cook for 15 minutes until reduced and slightly thickened. Transfer to a serving bowl, stir in the coriander and season to taste.

To make the fajitas, heat two tablespoons of the oil in a large frying pan and gently fry the onion and peppers for 6-8 minutes over a low heat until softened, stirring occasionally. Tip into a bowl.

Heat the remaining one tablespoon of oil in the same pan, add the beef strips and then sprinkle over the fajita seasoning mix, stirring to combine. Sauté for 6-8 minutes until cooked though and lightly golden.

Finely grate the rind from one of the limes and then squeeze out the juice. Cut the remaining lime into wedges and set aside to use as a garnish. Return the onion and pepper mixture to the pan with the lime juice and rind. Sauté for another 2-3 minutes until well combined and heated through. Season to taste.

Meanwhile, make the guacamole. Peel, stone and mash the avocados in a bowl. Add the onion, garlic, chilli, tomatoes, coriander, lime rind and juice. Mix well to combine and season to taste.

Heat a frying or griddle pan. Add a soft flour tortilla and heat for 30 seconds, turning once until soft and pliable. Repeat with the remaining tortillas and stack them up on a warmed plate.

To Serve Transfer the spicy beef mixture into a serving bowl and garnish with the lime wedges. Hand around the tomato salsa, tortillas, guacamole, soured cream and chopped spring onions, allowing each person to assemble the fajitas themselves.

Tip If you like your food hot double the amount of jalapeño peppers and leave the seeds in the fresh chilli.

Duck Breasts with Cabbage and Wild Mushroom Stir Fry

Serves 4

This has to be one of my favourite dishes using duck, as the cabbage and wild mushroom stir fry complements the duck perfectly and the five spice balsamic cream helps to cut through the richness of the dish. I like to use free-range Peking duck breasts, which I am lucky enough to have a regular supply of from Ken Moffitt at Thornhill Farm. Find them in Dublin in Caviston's, Downey's, O'Tooles and McKiernan's. Otherwise you'll get Peking duck in the supermarket. They just won't be free-range.

Ingredients

4 x 6oz / 175g duck breasts
2 tablespoons olive oil
1oz / 25g unsalted butter

For the Five Spice Balsamic Cream

1/4 pint / 150ml cream
1/4 pint / 150ml beef or duck stock
1 teapsoon Chinese five spice powder
1 tablespoon tomato purée
about 2 tablespoons balsamic vinegar

For the Cabbage & Wild Mushroom Stir Fry

12oz / 350g Savoy cabbage, finely sliced
75g / 3oz unsalted butter
1 small red onion, thinly sliced
2 garlic cloves, finely chopped
6oz / 175g mixed wild mushrooms, sliced
salt and freshly ground black pepper

Method Preheat the oven to 190C/375F/Gas 5. Trim the excess fat from duck breasts, leaving the skin in place. Make a few shallow, diagonal cuts across the skin-side of each breast with a sharp knife, taking care not to cut down into the flesh, then season.

Heat an ovenproof frying pan until very hot. Add the oil and then the duck breasts, skin-side down, and cook for about 3 minutes until crisp and lightly browned. Turn over and cook for another minute to seal in the juices. Add the butter to the frying pan, slide it into the oven and leave them to roast for about 5-7 minutes if you like your duck pink, or a little longer if you prefer it well done.

To make the five spice balsamic cream, put the cream, stock, Chinese five spice powder, tomato purée and balsamic vinegar into a small pan. Bring to the boil and cook for about 5 minutes until reduced and thickened to a sauce consistency. Season well and keep warm.

Meanwhile, make the cabbage and wild mushroom stir fry. Place the cabbage and 2-3 tablespoons of water into a large pan and cook over a high heat for a couple of minutes until only just tender and still crunchy. Tip onto a plate and set aside. Add the butter to the pan, and once it has melted add the onion and garlic and cook for 4-5 minutes until soft and lightly browned. Add the mushrooms and stir fry for 2 minutes until just tender. Add the cabbage, stir well and cook gently until heated through. Season to taste and keep warm.

To Serve Remove the duck breasts from oven and leave to rest for about 5 minutes, then carve each one across into thin slices, keeping them in shape. Spoon the cabbage and wild mushroom stir fry into the centre of each warmed serving plate. Slide a palette knife under each duck breast and lift them on top of the stir fry. Pour the five spice balsamic cream around the edge of each plate.

Tip Don't be tempted to wash mushrooms, as they will just soak up the water like a sponge. The best way of cleaning them is to gently brush away any dirt and/or grit with a fine pastry or paint brush.

Thai Turkey Stir Fry with Noodles

Serves 4

This noodle stir fry is the backbone of any number of simple suppers. Once you have mastered the technique, recipes are not necessary - just use your judgement with whatever vegetables you have to hand. But remember this is not a dumping ground for everything left in the fridge. Keep the flavours simple and clean and you should achieve excellent results every time.

Ingredients
2oz / 50g cashew nuts
12oz / 350g medium Chinese egg noodles
2 teaspoons toasted sesame oil
2 tablespoons vegetable oil
2 garlic cloves, crushed
1 teaspoon finely grated fresh root ginger
1 mild red chilli, seeded and thinly sliced
1lb / 450g turkey breast fillet, cut into small strips
1 courgette, trimmed and cut into sticks
1 yellow and one red pepper, seeded and sliced
4oz / 100g baby corn, halved
1 tablespoon light soy sauce
1 tablespoon sweet chilli sauce
2-3 tablespoons chopped fresh coriander
salt and freshly ground black pepper

Method Heat a frying pan over a medium heat. Toast the cashew nuts for 4-5 minutes, tossing the pan occasionally to prevent them from burning. Tip into a bowl and set aside.

Plunge the noodles in a pan of boiling salted water, then remove from the heat and set aside for 4 minutes until tender or according to packet instructions. Drain, then toss in half of the sesame oil and set aside. Keep warm.

Meanwhile, heat a wok until it is very hot. Add the vegetable oil and swirl up the sides. Add the garlic, ginger and chilli and cook for just 30 seconds. Add the turkey and stir fry for 2-3 minutes until well sealed and lightly coloured. Add the courgette, peppers and baby corn and stir fry for another 4-5 minutes or until the vegetables are tender but still crunchy.

Add the reserved toasted cashew nuts to the wok with the soy sauce, sweet chilli sauce and coriander, then toss briefly to combine. Season to taste and sprinkle over the remaining teaspoon of sesame oil.

To Serve Arrange the noodles on warmed serving plates and then spoon the turkey stir fry on top.

Tip This recipe also works well with strips of lean lamb or pork, or with whole peeled raw tiger prawns although these will just need to be added in at the last minute to prevent overcooking.

Chicken Korma

Serves 4

This recipe was very kindly given to me by my good friend Naseem Booth with whom I am lucky enough to work at Fermanagh College where I continue to teach. The spicing is absolutely authentic so it won't resemble the formula restaurant version. Apparently it is traditionally the Emperor's favourite and now one of mine too. In India it would be garnished with silver foil and fresh rose petals, but for me it needs nothing more than a scattering of fresh coriander leaves.

Ingredients

2 tablespoons vegetable oil
2 onions, finely chopped
2 garlic cloves, crushed
2 teaspoons finely grated root ginger
1 green chilli, seeded and chopped finely (optional)
1 teaspoon garam masala
1 teaspoon ground turmeric
1/4 teaspoon chilli powder
14oz / 400g can chopped tomatoes
1 teaspoon tomato puree
4 boneless skinless chicken breasts, cut into 1in / 2.5cm cubes
1/4 pint / 150ml cream
2 tablespoons roughly chopped fresh coriander
salt and freshly ground black pepper
cooked basmati rice (page 71), warmed naan bread and mango chutney, to serve

Method Heat the oil in a pan and fry the onions and garlic for about 10 minutes until golden brown. Stir in the ginger and green chilli, if using, and cook for 1 minute, stirring.

Add the garam masala to the pan with the turmeric, chilli powder and a pinch of salt and cook for another minute, stirring. Add the tomatoes, tomato puree and 1/4 pint / 150ml of water, stir well to combine, then reduce the heat and simmer for 20-25 minutes until the sauce is so well reduced that is almost sticking to the bottom of the pan and the oil has separated out on the surface, stirring occasionally.

Add the chicken to the pan with a few tablespoons of water to the reduced down sauce. Slowly bring to the boil, then reduce the heat and simmer gently for about 20 minutes or until the chicken is cooked through and completely tender. Stir in the cream and simmer gently for another few minutes until well combined. Season to taste.

To Serve Arrange the basmati rice and chicken korma on warmed serving plates and scatter over the coriander. Place the naan breads in a separate serving dish to pass around at the table along with the mango chutney.

Tip For a healthier option, omit the cream - you will still have a wonderfully fragrant plain chicken curry.

Turkey and Leek Pie

Serves 4-6

These pies are great served with my roasted garlic mash (page 35), buttered new potatoes or a simple lightly dressed salad. They are a brilliant way to use up leftover turkey or chicken and really are very simple to prepare. You could also make individual pies in 300ml/½ pint dishes; just decrease the cooking time to 25-30 minutes.

Ingredients

2oz / 50g butter, plus extra for greasing
1 onion, sliced
2 garlic cloves, sliced
1 large leek, trimmed and sliced
9oz / 250g button mushrooms, sliced
1 tablespoon plain flour, plus extra for dusting
9fl oz / 250ml chicken stock
3½fl oz / 100ml cream
1 bay leaf
3 tablespoons chopped fresh parsley
2lb / 900g cooked turkey breast, cut into bite-sized pieces
7-8oz / 200-225g ready rolled puff pastry, thawed if frozen
1 egg, lightly beaten
salt and freshly ground black pepper
Roasted garlic mash (page 35) and buttered peas, to serve (optional)

Method Preheat the oven to 190C/375F/Gas 5.

Heat the butter in pan. Add the onion, garlic, leek and mushrooms and sauté for 2-3 minutes until softened but not coloured. Stir in the flour and cook for 2 minutes, stirring continuously.

Gradually pour the stock into the pan followed by the cream, stirring until smooth after each addition. Add the bay leaf, bring to the boil and then reduce the heat and simmer for 5 minutes until thickened and slightly reduced, stirring occasionally. Stir in the parsley, season to taste and set aside to cool. Cover with a buttered circle of non-stick parchment paper to prevent a skin forming.

Place the cooked turkey into a 3 pint / 1.75 litre pie dish and ladle over the leek sauce. Stir gently to combine. Roll out the pastry to a 0.5cm/¼in thickness on a lightly floured work surface to an oval that will fit the top of the pie dish, making sure that it is large enough to hang over the edges like a 'blanket'.

Place the pastry lid on top of the pie, trimming it down to fit and brush around the edges with a little water to help it stick, then press down along the sides to seal. Cut a small slit in the pie lid to allow the steam to escape and with the trimmings of the pastry you could cut out a few leaves to decorate the top. Brush with the beaten egg and bake for 45 minutes to 1 hour or until the pastry is puffed up and golden brown.

To Serve Place the pie on the table and allow people to help themselves on to warmed serving plates with some of the roasted garlic mash and peas, if liked.

Tip Replace the cooked turkey with raw turkey or chicken and dust in two tablespoons of seasoned flour. Sauté until tender, then remove from the pan and prepare the sauce as described above. Return to the pan once the sauce has been made and allow to simmer until tender. Continue as above.

Spicy Chicken Salad with Avocado Salsa

Serves 4

Delicious succulent pieces of chicken coated in crisp spicy breadcrumbs and served with an avocado salsa that is flavoured at the last minute with some of my balsamic cream is a real winner with kids. It makes a perfect lunch or supper on a warm summers day.

Ingredients

8 slices white bread, crusts removed (1 day old)
1 tablespoon medium curry powder
1 tablespoon chilli powder
1 tablespoon sesame seeds
2 tablespoons chopped fresh parsley
2oz / 50g plain flour
1 egg
1 tablespoon milk
2 boneless skinless large chicken breasts, cut into strips lengthways
sunflower oil, for deep-frying
1oz / 25g mixed baby salad leaves

For the Avocado Salsa

1 avocado, peeled, stone removed and diced
1 tomato, seeded and diced
1 yellow pepper, seeded and diced
1 small red onion, finely chopped
1 garlic clove, crushed
1 tablespoon chopped fresh mixed herbs (such as chives and coriander)
juice of 1 lime
3½fl oz / 4fl oz extra virgin olive oil

For the Balsamic Cream

¼ pint / 150ml cream
¼ pint / 150ml beef or chicken stock
1 tablespoon tomato puree
about 2 tablespoons balsamic vinegar
salt and freshly ground black pepper

Method To make the avocado salsa, cut the avocado in half and remove the stone, then scoop out the flesh and cut into dice. Place in a bowl and add the tomato, pepper, onion, garlic, herbs, lime juice and olive oil. Season to taste and stir well to combine. Cover with clingfilm and leave at room temperature for up to 30 minutes to allow the flavours to develop.

Place the bread in a food processor or liquidiser and whiz to fine crumbs, then with the motor still running add the curry powder, chilli powder, sesame seeds and parsley until combined. Tip into a dish and season.

Place the flour on a plate and then beat the egg and milk together in another shallow dish. Toss the chicken strips into the flour until well coated, shaking off any excess, then dip into the egg mixture and then coat in the flavoured breadcrumbs.

Heat the a deep-fat fryer to 180C/350F or half fill a deep-sided pan with the sunflower oil. Cook the breaded chicken strips for 4-5 minutes or until cooked through and golden brown - you may have to do this in batches. Drain on kitchen paper and keep warm, if necessary.

Meanwhile, make the balsamic cream. Place the cream, stock, tomato puree and balsamic vinegar into a small pan. Bring to the boil and cook for about 5 minutes until reduced and thickened to a sauce consistency. Season well and keep warm.

To Serve Pile the spicy chicken into a warmed serving bowl and place on the table with the bowl avocado salsa. Pour the balsamic cream into a jug and allow people to help themselves.

Tip For a dinner party, spoon the salsa into 4in / 10cm cooking rings set on serving plates and ladle some of the balsamic cream around each one. Arrange the spicy chicken on top and top with the salad leaves.

Roast Chicken and Pumpkin Risotto

Serves 4

This risotto is a great recipe to use up leftover roast chicken or turkey, especially at Christmas when after all the seasonal excesses you tend to be craving something different. If pumpkin is not available try using butternut squash which has an excellent flavour and isn't seasonal.

Ingredients
sunflower oil, for deep and shallow frying
4 boneless chicken thighs
1½oz / 40g butter
1 small onion, diced
1 baby leek, diced
4oz / 100g slice pumpkin, peeled, seeded and diced
1 large carrot, diced
2 pints / 1.2 litres chicken stock
12oz / 350g arborio rice (risotto)
1 tablespoon Mascarpone cheese
1 tablespoon freshly grated Parmesan
2 potatoes
2 tablespoons chopped fresh mixed herbs (such as basil and parsley)
salt and freshly ground black pepper

Method Preheat the oven to 180C/350F/Gas 4. Heat an ovenproof frying pan. Add a thin film of oil and then add the chicken, skin-side down. Cook for 4 minutes until crisp and golden brown, then turn over and transfer to the oven to roast for another 10-15 minutes until tender and cooked through. Cool, then remove and discard the skin and dice the flesh. Place in a bowl, cover with clingfilm and chill until needed.

Heat a sauté pan over a medium heat. Melt the butter, and then add the onion, leek, pumpkin and carrot and sauté for about 5 minutes until almost tender and just starting to colour, stirring occasionally.

Pour the stock into a separate pan and bring to a simmer. Stir the rice into the onion mixture and cook for a minute or two, stirring until all the grains are well coated. Ladle in about 150ml/¼ pint of the hot stock, stirring to combine, then lower the heat to a simmer, and cook, stirring almost continuously, until all the stock has been absorbed. Repeat until nearly all of the stock has been used up and the rice is 'al dente'. This should take no more than 20 minutes.

Stir the reserved chicken into the cooked risotto and allow to just warm through. Add the mascarpone cheese, Parmesan and herbs and mix well to combine. Season to taste.

Heat a deep-fat fryer until 190C/375F or half fill a deep-sided pan with sunflower oil. Peel the potatoes and then thinly slice on a mandolin or use a food processor with the correct attachment blade (it's a bit more difficult by hand using a very sharp knife). Dry the potato slices well and then tip into the heated oil and cook for 2-3 minutes until cooked through and golden brown, stirring with a slotted spoon to help them cook evenly. Drain well on kitchen paper and season with salt.

To Serve Spoon the risotto on to large warmed serving plates and garnish with the deep-fried potato slices.

Tip The risotto is cooked when the grains of rice are 'al dente', tender but still with a little bit of a bite, and the consistency should be creamy and loose, not at all thick. The moment you are happy with the texture, enrich with the mascarpone and Parmesan and herbs and season to taste. Serve immediately.

Chicken Rocket and Pine Nut Pasta

Serves 2

The sauce for this recipe literally takes the time the pasta needs to cook. It uses rocket or watercess, of which I get a regular supply from Rod Alston at Eden Plants, one of the best organic farms in Ireland. I'm just so lucky that it's only five minutes up the road from the restaurant, but thankfully organic vegetables are becoming easier to find. There is now a wider range of good quality pasta available, but without a doubt my favourite is *De Cecco* that comes in blue packets and is now available in most larger supermarkets and good delis.

Ingredients
8oz / 225g penne pasta
3 tablespoons pine nuts
3 tablespoons olive oil
2 boneless skinless large chicken breasts, sliced lengthways into thin strips (about 8oz / 225g in total)
1 onion, thinly sliced
2 garlic cloves, crushed
1 teaspoon fresh thyme leaves
1 tablespoon wholegrain mustard
1/4 pint / 150ml cream
4 1/2oz / 125g wild rocket or watercress
about 4 teaspoons chilli oil (shop bought or homemade page 27)
salt and freshly ground black pepper
Parmesan shavings, to garnish

Method Plunge the penne into a large pan of boiling salted water and cook for about 10 minutes until 'al dente' or according to packet instructions.

Heat a frying pan over a medium heat and add the pine nuts. Cook for a few minutes until lightly toasted, tossing occasionally to prevent them from burning. Tip into a bowl and set aside.

Add two tablespoons of the oil to the frying pan and sauté the onion, garlic and thyme for 2-3 minutes until softened and just beginning to colour. Tip into a bowl and set side.

Add the remaining tablespoon of oil to the frying pan and then add the chicken strips. Cook for 2-3 minutes and season lightly, then turn over and cook for another 2-3 until cooked through and lightly golden.

Return the onion mixture to the frying pan, stirring until well combined. Stir in the mustard and cream and then bring to a gentle simmer. Cook for 1 minute to just heat through, but do not allow the mixture to boil.

Drain the pasta and quickly refresh, then return to the pan. Pour in the creamy chicken mixture and add the rocket or watercress. Toss lightly together to combine and season to taste.

To Serve Spoon the pasta on to warmed serving plates and then sprinkle over the toasted pine nuts. Drizzle over the chilli or olive oil and garnish with the Parmesan shavings.

Tip Parmesan shavings are now sold in small cartons in some supermarkets, but it really is very easy to make your own; just pare a block of good quality Parmesan with a vegetable peeler - it's as simple as that!

Coq Au Vin

Serves 6

This classic French coq au vin uses a whole oven-ready chicken that I chop into portions. Serve with my roasted garlic mash (page 35) to mop up all the juices and some crisp steamed broccoli.

Ingredients
4lb / 1.75kg oven-ready chicken
2-3 tablespoons vegetable oil
6oz / 175g piece smoked bacon, cut into strips
1 onion, sliced
2 carrots, sliced
2 celery stalks, sliced
2 garlic cloves, finely chopped
1 bottle red wine
2 teaspoons chopped fresh thyme
16fl oz / 500ml chicken stock
2oz / 50g butter
20 baby pearl onions or small shallots
9oz / 250g button mushrooms, quartered
2 tsp cornflour (optional)
1 tablespoon chopped fresh parsley
salt and freshly ground black pepper
Heart shaped croutons, to garnish (see tip - optional)

Method To cut the chicken into portions, place on a board and holding the breasts firmly, cut off the end joint of the drumsticks and the parson's nose. Cut along one side of the breastbone from the body cavity to the neck cavity. Spread open and cut along both sides of the backbone to remove it. Lay the chicken halves, skin-side up, on the board and cut diagonally between the breast and leg joints. Cut in half again to make eight potions, discarding the chicken carcass or use it for stock.

Heat one tablespoon of the vegetable oil in a casserole dish with a lid over a medium heat. Add the bacon and sauté for 3-4 minutes until lightly browned. Tip into a bowl and set aside. Add a little more oil to the pan and half of the chicken skin-side down and cook for 6-8 minutes until golden brown, turning once. Transfer onto a plate and repeat, adding a little more oil if necessary.

Add the onion to the casserole dish with the carrots, celery and garlic and sauté for about 5 minutes until golden brown. Pour in the red wine, add the thyme and bring to a simmer, then cook for 5 minutes, scraping the bottom of the pan with a wooden spoon to remove any sediment. Pour in the stock and then add the chicken. Cover and simmer for about 1 hour or until the chicken is cooked through and tender.

Meanwhile, melt 1oz / 25g of the butter in a frying pan. Add the pearl onions or shallots and sauté for 5 minutes. Tip into the bowl with the reserved bacon. Add the remaining butter to the pan and once it stops foaming, tip in the mushrooms. Sauté for 5 minutes until tender. Add to the bacon mixture and set aside.

When the chicken is cooked, carefully transfer to a large plate and set aside. Strain the sauce into a clean pan, discarding the vegetables. If you'd like a thicker sauce, mix the cornflour with a little water and then whisk into the sauce and simmer for a few minutes until thickened, whisking occasionally. Add the bacon-mixture, stir to combine and simmer for 10 minutes to allow the flavours to combine. Return the chicken to the casserole and cook for another 5 minutes until heated through. Season to taste.

To Serve Transfer the coq au vin to a warmed serving dish and sprinkle over the parsley. Garnish with the heart shaped croutons, if liked and serve straight from the table on to warmed serving plates.

Tip Stamp or cut out heart shapes from slices of white bread and fry in a little oil until golden brown. Remove from the pan with a tongs and immediately dip the end points into chopped fresh parsley to coat.

Seared Tuna with Roasted Red Pepper Salsa

Serves 4

When chargrilling the tuna fillets don't be tempted to fiddle with them: you are looking to get nice dark griddle lines. This also helps to caramelise the tuna's juices and produces a tastier fillet. Try to remove the tuna from the fridge 15 minutes before using so that it not still cold in the middle after being cooked. If you can keep the portion size down, this also makes an exquisite starter.

Ingredients
2 x 6oz / 175g tuna loin fillets
2 tablespoons olive oil

For the Roasted Red Pepper Salsa
1 large red pepper
1 tablespoon chilli oil (page 27 - or extra virgin olive oil)
1 garlic clove, crushed
1 medium-hot red chilli, seeded and finely chopped
juice of 1 lime
1 tablespoon chopped fresh mixed herbs (such as coriander and parsley)
salt and freshly ground black pepper
fresh coriander sprigs, to garnish
fresh green salad, to serve

Method To make the roasted red pepper salsa, you can roast the pepper in one of two ways. Spear the stalk end of the pepper on a fork and turn it over the flame of a gas flame on the hob, or use a blowtorch, turning regularly until the skin has blistered and blackened. Alternatively, preheat the oven to 220C/425F/Gas 7 and roast in a small roasting tin for 20-25 minutes until the skin is black. Leave to cool and then break in half and remove the stalk, skin and seeds; discard. Cut the flesh into small dice and place in a bowl.

Put the chilli or olive oil, garlic and red chilli into a small pan and as soon as it starts to sizzle, pour it on to the roasted red pepper dice, mixing well to combine. Add the lime juice, herbs and season to taste. Transfer to a serving bowl and set aside.

Heat a griddle or heavy-based frying pan over a medium heat until very hot. Brush the tuna fillets all over with the olive oil and then season. Add to the pan and cook for 2 minutes on each side, if you like your tuna still a little rare in the middle. Cook for a few minutes longer if you prefer it more well done.

To Serve Arrange the seared tuna fillets on warmed serving plates and spoon some of the roasted red pepper salsa alongside, placing the remainder on the table for people to help themselves. Garnish with the coriander sprigs and serve the salad in a separate bowl on the table.

Tip Once the red pepper is roasted place it in a bowl and cover tightly with clingfilm and then allow to cool. This will help steam off the skin so that is peels off easily.

Herb and Nut Crusted Cod Fillets

Serves 4

This dish is a great dinner party staple as most of the work can be done well in advance and it looks and tastes fantastic. Cod is one of my favourite fish for roasting in the oven. It cooks firm and succulent, has excellent flavour, but you could also use haddock or salmon fillets.

Ingredients
3oz / 75g butter
8 slices wholemeal bread, crusts removed (1 day old)
2oz / 50g walnut halves, roughly chopped
6 tablespoons chopped fresh mixed herbs (such as parsley and chives)
finely grated rind of 1 orange
pinch fresh grated nutmeg
2 limes, sliced
4 x 6oz / 175g cod fillets, boned (each at least 1in / 2.5cm thick)
1 egg yolk, beaten
4 small vines of cherry tomatoes (about 8 on each one)
about 1 tablespoon olive oil

For the Tartare Sauce
½ pint/ 300ml mayonnaise (fresh or from a jar is fine)
1oz / 25g capers, well rinsed and chopped
1oz / 25g gherkins, well rinsed and chopped
juice of ½ lemon
1 teaspoon snipped fresh chives
salt and freshly ground black pepper

Method Preheat the oven to 200C/400F/Gas 6.

Melt the butter in a small pan or in the microwave and leave to cool. Place the bread in a food processor or liquidiser and whiz to fine crumbs. Tip into a bowl and stir the cooled butter, walnuts, herbs, orange rind and nutmeg. Season to taste and mix well to combine.

Arrange the lime slices in four groups on a baking sheet and place the cod fillets on top, skin-side down. Season and brush over the egg yolk.

Divide the flavoured crumbs on top of the cod fillets and then spread them out, pressing them down firmly to stick. Arrange the tomatoes vines around the crusted cod fillets and drizzle each one with a little of the oil. Bake for 15-20 minutes until the cod is cooked through and the crumbs are crisp and golden, and the tomatoes have softened and are lightly charred.

Meanwhile, make the tartare sauce. Place the mayonnaise in a serving bowl and stir in the capers, gherkins, lemon juice and chives until well combined. Season to taste, cover with clingfilm and chill until ready to use. This will sit happily in the fridge for up to 2 days.

To Serve Using a fish slice, transfer the crusted cod fillets and lime slices on to warmed serving plates. Add a vine of the roasted cherry tomatoes to each one, along with a good spoonful of the tartare sauce, serving the remainder separately at the table for people to help themselves.

Tip Lightly toasted pine nuts or chopped blanched almonds would also work brilliantly in this dish instead of walnuts.

Spicy Monkfish Kebabs with Salsa Verde

Serves 4

Salsa verde is a great Italian sauce that goes wonderfully with these monkfish kebabs that have been marinated with plenty of gutsy flavours. The salsa really does need to taste very fresh, so don't make it too far in advance. I always think it tastes better when it's chopped by hand, using a large sharp knife, but you can always pulse it in the food processor if you are short of time.

Ingredients
5 tablespoons olive oil
1 garlic clove, crushed
3fl oz / 85ml dark soy sauce
1 teaspoon finely grated fresh root ginger
1 teaspoon caster sugar
1 tablespoon sweet chilli sauce
2¼lb / 1kg monkfish fillets, trimmed and cut into 1¼in / 3cm cubes

For the Salsa Verde
2 handfuls fresh parsley leaves or sprigs (no stalks)
1 tablespoon rinsed capers
4 canned anchovy fillets, well drained
1 garlic clove, peeled
1 teaspoon Dijon mustard
1 tablespoon fresh lemon juice
2fl oz / 50ml extra virgin olive oil
salt and freshly ground black pepper
egg noodles, to serve
lime wedges, to garnish (optional)

Method Place four tablespoons of the olive oil in a shallow large non-metallic dish and add the garlic, soy, ginger, sugar and sweet chilli sauce. Season to taste and mix well to combine. Add the monkfish cubes, turning to coat and then cover with clingfilm and chill for 2-3 hours. This time allows the flavours to develop.

To make salsa verde, finely chop the parsley with the capers, anchovies and garlic by hand, or pulse together in a food processor or liquidiser. Transfer to a non-metallic bowl and whisk in mustard, lemon juice and olive oil, or blend together in the food processor and then tip into a non-metallic bowl. Season to taste, cover with clingfilm and set aside at room temperature to allow the flavours to develop - up to 30 minutes is fine.

Heat a large non-stick heavy-based frying pan over a medium heat until very hot. Thread the marinated monkfish cubes on to 12 x 6in / 15cm bamboo or metal skewers, reserving any remaining marinade. Add the remaining tablespoon of oil to the pan and then add the skewers. Cook for 8-10 minutes until cooked through and lightly charred, turning regularly and basting with the remaining marinade.

To Serve Arrange three kebabs in the centre of each warmed serving plate and serve with egg noodles. Divide the salsa verde among small ramekins and set to the side. Garnish with the lime wedges if desired.

● **Tip** Fresh root ginger that has been peeled freezes very well and can be grated straight from frozen. This means that there is no danger of it drying out and going woody before you've had a chance to use it.

Skate with Lemon and Caper Butter Sauce

Serves 4

Skate (or ray as it is sometimes known) is a very undervalued fish in this country. It's hard to understand why as it is always so competitively priced, has a lovely delicate texture with no tiny bones to worry about. I find them particularly succulent served on the bone as the flesh stays moist and full of flavour. This recipe is just so simple to make and needs little or no preparation.

Ingredients
2 tablespoons olive oil
1oz / 25g plain flour
1 tsp coarsely ground black pepper
4 x 7oz / 200g skate wings, skinned
4oz / 100g butter
10oz / 300g baby leeks, trimmed and cut into 3in / 7.5cm lengths
pinch caster sugar

For the Lemon and Caper Butter Sauce
4fl oz / 120ml cream
1 garlic clove,
crushed juice of 1 lemon
2oz / 50g capers, well rinsed (small, if possible)
4oz / 100g butter, diced and well chilled
1 tablespoon chopped fresh parsley
salt and freshly ground black pepper

Method Heat a large heavy-based frying pan and add a tablespoon of the olive oil. Place the flour on a plate and the coarsely ground black pepper, then mix well to combine. Lightly dust two of the skate wings in the seasoned flour, shaking off any excess. Add 1oz / 25g of the butter to the frying pan and as soon as it starts foaming, cook the dusted skate wings for about 4-5 minutes on each side until lightly golden, depending on their thickness. Transfer to a hot plate and keep warm while you cook the rest, first dusting them in seasoned flour and then cooking them in the remaining tablespoon of oil and 1oz/ 25g of the butter.

Meanwhile, place the baby leeks in a pan with a lid and add the remaining 2oz / 50g of the butter, the sugar and a tablespoon of water. Cover and bring to the boil, then boil fast for about 3 minutes until the leeks are completely tender and all of the liquid has evaporated, shaking the pan occasionally to ensure even cooking. Season to taste and keep warm, but be careful not to overcook.

To make the lemon and caper butter sauce, place the cream in a small pan with the garlic, lemon juice and capers and bring to a gentle simmer. Cook for 4-5 minutes until slightly reduced and thickened, whisking occasionally. Gradually whisk in the pieces of chilled butter, a few at a time, until you have achieved a light emulsion. Whisk in the parsley and then season to taste.

To Serve Arrange the skate in the centre of warmed serving plates and spoon over the lemon and caper butter sauce. Garnish with the baby leeks.

Tip When buying skate, freshness is the most important quality to look for, so buy from a reliable fishmonger. As it is quite a slimy fish it tastes best on the day it was caught. If you are lucky enough to find it spanking fresh I promise you'll understand what all the fuss is about.

Salmon and Asparagus Wraps with Sun-Dried Tomato Dressing

Serves 6

Farmed salmon has become much better quality over the years and in my opinion some of the best available comes from Ireland where sea is always freezing cold and for the most part unpolluted with strong tidal flows. Make sure your salmon fillets are all even-sized and about 1in /2.5cm thick to ensure even cooking. They also work well on the barbecue and can be prepared up to 12 hours in advance, covered with clingfilm and chilled until needed - just don't add the squeeze of lemon juice until you are ready to cook them.

Ingredients
9 asparagus spears, trimmed and halved lengthways
6 x 6oz / 175g skinless salmon fillets (each about 1in / 2.5cm thick)
small bunch fresh dill, stalks removed, plus sprigs reserved to garnish
6 slices Parma ham
1/2 lemon, pips removed
1 tablespoon olive oil
1oz / 25g butter

For the Sun-Dried Tomato Dressing
12 semi sun-dried tomatoes, roughly chopped
7fl oz / 200ml extra virgin olive oil
1 tsp fresh lemon juice
pinch chilli powder
3 fresh basil leaves
salt and freshly ground black pepper
lightly dressed wild rocket leaves, to serve

Method Preheat the oven to 190C/375F/Gas 5.

To make the semi sun-dried tomato dressing, place the sun-dried tomatoes in a food processor or liquidiser with the olive oil, lemon juice, chilli powder and basil leaves and blend for about 1 minute until you have achieved a fairly smooth texture. Transfer to a bowl and season to taste. Cover with clingfilm and chill until ready to use - this can be made up to 24 hours in advance.

Blanch the asparagus spears in a pan of boiling salted water for 1 minute. Drain and quickly refresh, then tip into a bowl of ice-cold water to cool completely. Drain well and pat dry on kitchen paper.

Season each salmon fillet and arrange three asparagus spears, trimming them down as necessary and a few dill fronds on top of each one. Lightly wrap a slice of Parma ham around each bundle and place in a shallow non-metallic dish. Drizzle over a little of the dressing and add a squeeze of lemon juice.

Heat the olive oil in a large ovenproof frying pan and add the butter. Once it stops foaming, add the salmon wraps presentation-side down and cook for 2 minutes on each side to seal. Transfer to the oven and roast for another 10 minutes, turning once, until the salmon wraps are cooked through and golden brown.

To Serve Arrange the salmon wraps on warmed serving plates. Quickly whisk the dressing until combined and then spoon on top. Garnish with the reserved dill sprigs. Place a small mound of the rocket leaves to the side.

Tip Semi sun-dried tomatoes are really worth tracking down as they really do have the most fantastic intense almost sweet flavour. Look out for them in the supermarket in small cartons from the chilled section with the dips or from the deli counter. Obviously good delis also stock them as do all the numerous food markets that operate around the country.

Tagliatelle with Salmon and Prawns

Serves 4

Flavour-packed, this is a lovely fresh tasting pasta dish perfect for lazy al fresco meals in the summer. The sauce can be made well in advance and just reheated gently when the pasta is almost cooked. Serve it as a main course lunch with hunks of warm crusty Italian bread to mop up all those delicious juices and some well-chilled crisp white wine.

Ingredients

12oz / 350g salmon fillet, bones removed and skin left on
$^1/_4$ pint / 150ml dry white wine
12 fresh basil sprigs
$^1/_4$ pint / 150ml cream
2 teaspoons tomato puree
1 garlic clove, crushed
12oz / 350g tagliatelle
4oz / 100g cooked peeled tiger prawns, thawed if frozen
6 plum tomatoes, peeled, seeded and finely chopped
$^1/_2$ lemon, pips removed
salt and freshly ground black pepper
warm crusty Italian bread, to serve (optional)

Method Place the salmon skin-side up in a sauté pan with a lid and pour over the wine. Tuck in four basil sprigs and season the salmon. Bring to the boil and cover, then reduce the heat and simmer gently for 5-7 minutes or until the salmon is just tender and cooked through. Remove from the heat and set the salmon aside to cool completely in the liquid.

When the salmon has cooled, remove from the pan and flake the flesh into large chunks, discarding the skin and bones. Place in a bowl and set aside. Add the cream, the poaching liquid with the tomato puree and garlic. Bring to the boil, stirring well to combine and then reduce the heat and simmer uncovered for 10-15 minutes until well reduced to a sauce consistency, stirring occasionally.

Meanwhile, cook the tagliatelle in a large pan of boiling salted water for 8-10 minutes or according to packet instructions until 'al dente'. When the pasta is almost ready add the flaked salmon to the reduced down sauce with the prawns and tomato dice, then add a squeeze of the lemon juice and tear in six of the basil sprigs and allow to just heat through, gently shaking the pan occasionally. Season to taste.

To Serve Drain the pasta and quickly refresh. Tip into a warmed serving bowl. Pour over the sauce and toss gently to combine. Garnish with the four basil sprigs and serve straight on the table into warmed individual serving bowls. Put the warm crusty Italian bread in a separate bowl to hand around.

Tip I find the easiest way to remove the skins from tomatoes is to place them on a fork and put them directly into the gas flame on the hob, turning occasionally. The skins should blacken and split almost immediately, but the flesh will still be completely firm and not at all mushy. Of course, a blowtorch would produce exactly the same results.

Wild Mushroom Strudel

Serves 4-6

This is a very impressive vegetarian main course that contains the wonderful combination of sautéed mushrooms and a crisp pastry crust. The filo pastry helps to keep the mushroom mixture really moist and full of flavour. The strudel can be prepared several hours in advance as long as it is tightly covered with clingfilm in the fridge and just popped in the oven once your guests arrive.

Ingredients
2 tablespoons olive oil, plus extra for greasing
2 garlic cloves, crushed
1 small onion, finely chopped
8oz / 225g mixed wild mushrooms, roughly chopped
1 bunch spring onions, trimmed and chopped (about 6 in total)
2 tablespoons chopped fresh mixed herbs (such as basil, parsley and chives)
4-5 sheets filo pastry, thawed if frozen (about 100g / 4oz in total)
1 egg, beaten
salt and freshly ground black pepper
lightly dressed mixed salad leaves and warm crusty bread, to serve

Method Preheat the oven to 190C/375F/Gas 5.

Heat the olive oil in a large frying pan. Add the garlic, onion and mushrooms and cook over a high heat for 2-3 minutes until almost tender. Add the spring onions, herbs and seasoning to taste. Sauté for another minute until well combined and the spring onions are just tender. Leave to cool.

Unroll the sheets of filo pastry and place them one on top of the other on a work surface. Brush the surface of the top sheet of pastry with beaten egg and then spread over mushroom mixture to within 1½in / 4cm of the edges. Starting with one short edge, roll up the pastry like you would a Swiss roll, keeping the mushrooms in place as you go. Place the strudel seam-side down on a lightly greased baking sheet and brush once more with the rest of the beaten egg. Bake for 15-20 minutes until crisp and golden brown.

To Serve Cut the strudel across into thick slices on the diagonal and arrange on warmed serving plates with some dressed mixed salad leaves and crusty bread, if desired.

Tip Try to buy the authentic Greek filo pastry and there really is a world of difference. Look for it in good delis or try the frozen section of a large supermarket.

Roasted Vegetable Rice

Serves 4-6

This is a great dish if you have to keep both meat-eaters and vegetarians happy. Simply serve the rice with some chargrilled lamb or pork chops and a big dollop of a cucumber raita on the side wouldn't go amiss. To make one, mix some yoghurt with some grated or diced cucumber and a little finely chopped spring onion and chopped fresh mint. Season to taste.

Ingredients

2 courgettes, cut into chunks
1 yellow and 1 red pepper, seeded and cut into chunks
1 small fennel bulb, cut into 6 even-sized wedges
2 red onions, cut into wedges
1 aubergine, cut into chunks
3 tablespoons olive oil
3 ripe tomatoes, halved
1 tablespoon balsamic vinegar
3 garlic cloves, finely chopped
pinch dried chilli flakes
12oz / 350g basmati rice, well washed (see tip)
1 teaspoon ground turmeric
6oz / 175g Cheddar cheese, cut into cubes
salt and freshly ground black pepper
roughly chopped fresh coriander, to garnish

Method Preheat oven to 200C/400F/Gas 6.

Place the courgettes, peppers, fennel, red onions and aubergine into a large roasting tin. Drizzle over the olive oil, season generously and roast for 30 minutes or until the vegetables are almost tender and lightly charred. Remove the tin from the oven and stir in the tomatoes, then sprinkle over the balsamic vinegar, garlic and chilli flakes. Roast for another 15 minutes until all the vegetables are completely tender and lightly charred.

Bring a large pan of water with a tight fitting lid to the boil and add the turmeric and a good pinch of salt. Add the rice, bring back to a rolling boil and stir once. Boil for exactly 8 minutes. Check the rice - it should have a slight crunch - then drain well and return to the pan; cover with the lid. Leave to steam in its own heat undisturbed for another 10 minutes. Don't be tempted to peek at the rice before it's ready - lifting the lid allows all the steam heat to escape. Use a fork to fluff up the grains and then fold in the Cheddar.

To Serve Divide the rice and Cheddar mixture among warmed serving plates and spoon over the roasted vegetables, drizzling any remaining juices from the roasting tin on top. Garnish with the fresh coriander.

Tip To achieve consistently light fluffy basmati rice, always wash the rice first under cold water until the water runs clear, indicating that you've got rid of most of the loose starch clinging to the rice grains. I often cook too much rice as it keeps perfectly well in the fridge for a day or two. If you find that it's gone into one big lump, simply separate it as best you can with your fingers, or stir in a splash of oil before refrigerating it.

Spicy Chickpea and Sweet Potato Curry

Serves 4

This curry is a worthy partner to basmati rice (page 71). However, as the puris can literally be made in minutes don't make them too far in advance or they will begin to harden.

Ingredients

2 tablespoons vegetable oil
1 small onion, thinly sliced
1lb / 450g sweet potatoes, peeled and cut into 1/2in / 2cm slices (orange-fleshed, if possible)
2 garlic cloves, crushed
1 teaspoon finely chopped fresh root ginger
1 green chilli, seeded and finely chopped (optional)
1 teaspoon garam masala
1 teaspoon chilli powder
1 teaspoon ground turmeric
14oz / 400g can chopped tomatoes
1/2 pint / 300ml vegetable stock
14oz / 400g can of chickpeas, drained and rinsed
6oz / 175g spinach, washed and tough stalks removed
1 tablespoon chopped fresh coriander

For the Puris

6oz / 175g plain wholemeal flour, plus extra for dusting
sunflower oil, for deep-frying plus about 3 tablespoons extra
salt and freshly ground black pepper

Method Heat the oil in a large pan and add the sweet potatoes. Cook for 2-3 minutes until just beginning to colour, turning once. Transfer to a bowl and set aside. Add the onion to the pan and sauté for 2-3 minutes until softened and then add the garlic, ginger and chilli, if using, and cook for 1-2 minutes, stirring.

Add the garam masala to the pan with the chilli powder and ground turmeric and cook for another minute, stirring continuously. Add the tomatoes, stirring to combine, and bring to a gentle simmer. Cook for 15-20 minutes until well reduced and thickened, stirring occasionally to prevent the bottom sticking.

Pour the stock into the pan and then add the chickpeas and reserved sweet potato slices, stirring to combine. Simmer gently for another 30 minutes or until the liquid has reduced to a sauce consistency. Finally stir in the spinach and allow to just wilt down. Season to taste.

Meanwhile, make the puris. Place the flour, a good pinch of salt and a tablespoon of the sunflower oil in a bowl. Make a well in the centre and gradually add enough cold water to form a very stiff dough - you'll need about 3fl oz / 85ml in total. Turn out on to a lightly floured surface and knead well until smooth. Place in a lightly oiled bowl and cover with clingfilm. Set aside to rest for 15 minutes.

Heat a deep-fat fryer to 190C/375F or half fill a deep-sided pan with sunflower oil, then divide the dough into eight to ten pieces. Lightly oil the dough and roll each piece into a disc with a lightly oiled rolling pin. Deep-fry the puris one at a time for 1-2 minutes until cooked through and golden brown, using a slotted spoon to push them down in the oil as this helps them to puff up. Drain on kitchen paper and keep warm.

To Serve Spoon the chickpea and sweet potato curry into warmed serving bowls and garnish with the coriander. Place the plate of puris on the table and allow people to help themselves.

Tip To make your own vegetable stock, onions and carrots are pretty essential, while fennel and tarragon add good flavour, but beyond that use whatever vegetables you fancy.

Risotto Primavera

Serves 4

When making this dish, which appeals to children and adults alike, you can completely change the flavour by using different vegetables. Or if it doesn't have to be vegetarian try folding in 1lb / 450g of sliced grilled sausages just before serving. There is now such a wide range of good quality sausages available from supermarkets and specialist butchers. Choose from pork and leek, Toulouse, spicy or even wild boar and apple. Chorizo also works well, just sliced and fried in a little oil before adding to the risotto – it will also give a wonderful pink hue to the risotto.

Ingredients
2 tablespoons olive oil
2 carrots, diced
2 leeks, trimmed and diced
2 garlic cloves, crushed
pinch saffron strands
2 pints / 1.2 litres vegetable stock
12oz / 350g arborio rice (risotto)
1/4 pint / 150ml white wine
4 1/2oz / 125g fine green beans, halved
4oz / 100g peas (fresh or frozen is fine)
4 tablespoons chopped fresh mixed herbs (such as chives, tarragon and parsley)
2oz / 50g freshly grated Parmesan (optional)
salt and freshly ground black pepper

Method Heat the oil in a large sauté pan and gently fry the carrots, leeks, garlic and saffron over a low heat for 5 minutes until softened but not coloured, stirring occasionally. Bring the stock to a gentle simmer in a separate pan. Stir the rice into the vegetable and saffron mixture and cook for 1 minute, stirring until the grains are well coated in oil and almost transparent. Pour in the wine and allow to bubble down for 1 minute, stirring.

Add a ladleful of the simmering stock and cook until it has been completely absorbed, stirring continuously. Continue to add the stock a ladleful at a time, making sure that each time you add the stock the previous amount has already been absorbed. After 20 minutes the rice should be nearly cooked, so tip in the beans and peas into the remaining stock for 2 minutes before adding both the stock and the vegetables to the risotto. Check that the rice is 'al dente', then remove from the heat and stir in the herbs and Parmesan. Season to taste.

To Serve Spoon the risotto into warmed serving bowls.

Tip Use leftovers from this dish to make risotto cakes – crunchy on the outside and rich and creamy in the middle. Simply roll and flatten handfuls of cold risotto into patties. Coat in a mixture of breadcrumbs and freshly grated Parmesan before frying in butter until golden.

Butternut Squash and Pasta Bake

Serves 4

The roasted butternut squash adds texture to this pasta gratin, while the mascarpone cheese helps to keep everything really moist. There's this ongoing debate about which pasta is better - fresh or dried, and I can honestly say that I think dried is best in most recipes. It uses hard durum wheat, which when cooked gives that lovely 'bite' that we talk about when cooking pasta.

Ingredients

1 tablespoon olive oil
1oz / 25g butter, plus extra for greasing
1 butternut squash (about 1½lb / 675g in total)
4 fresh rosemary sprigs
1 red onion, sliced
6oz / 175g chestnut mushrooms, sliced
10oz / 300g penne pasta
9oz / 250g tub mascarpone cheese
2oz / 50g freshly grated Parmesan
1 tablespoon chopped fresh parsley
salt and freshly ground black pepper
lightly dressed fresh green salad, to serve

Method Preheat the oven to 200C/400F/Gas 6.

Place the oil and butter in a large roasting tin and heat for 3-4 minutes in the oven until the butter has melted.

Peel the butternut squash and then cut in half and remove seeds; discard. Cut flesh into bite-sized chunks and then tip them into the heated butter and oil, tossing to coat. Season to taste and roast for 20 minutes. Stir in the rosemary, onion and mushrooms until well combined and roast for another 10 minutes or until all the vegetables are tender and just beginning to char.

Cook the pasta in a large pan of boiling salted water for about 10 minutes or according to packet instructions until 'al dente'.

Remove the roasting tin from the oven and stir in two tablespoons of water, then stir in the mascarpone cheese. Drain the pasta and tip into the roasting tin, stirring to combine. Season to taste. Transfer to a buttered ovenproof dish and sprinkle over the Parmesan. Bake for another 10 minutes until bubbling and lightly golden.

To Serve Sprinkle the parsley over the butternut squash and pasta bake and place directly on the table, allowing people to help themselves on to warmed serving plates. Put the salad in a separate bowl on the table.

Tip This dish can be prepared several hours in advance and just popped into a preheated oven 180C/350F/Gas 4 from cold for 25-30 minutes or until heated through, then flashed under the grill until bubbling.

Pappardelle Pasta with Sun-dried Tomato Pesto

Serves 4

This pesto makes a nice change from your average basil pesto. It would also be delicious swirled into spinach soup, or try stuffing some underneath the skin of chicken breasts before cooking. I also like to use it as a dressing for salads or spread on to crostini and topped with bubbling mozzarella - need I go on . . .

Ingredients
2 tablespoons olive oil
1 large aubergine, chopped into 1in / 2.5cm pieces
1 red and 1 yellow pepper, seeded and cut into squares
2 garlic cloves, crushed
1 small red chilli, seeded and finely chopped
12oz / 350g pappardelle pasta
grated rind and juice of 1 lemon
6 tablespoons torn fresh basil, plus extra sprigs to garnish
2oz / 50g Gruyère cheese, finely grated

For the Sun-Dried Tomato Pesto
6oz / 175g semi sun-dried tomatoes, roughly chopped
2 garlic cloves, peeled
8 large fresh basil leaves
7fl oz / 200ml extra virgin olive oil
salt and freshly ground black pepper

Method Heat the olive oil in a large pan over a medium heat. Add the aubergine and sauté for about 5 minutes until tender. Add the peppers, garlic and chilli and seasoning to taste, then sauté for another 10 minutes until all the vegetables are completely tender.

Meanwhile, cook the pappardelle in a large pan of boiling salted water for 8-10 minutes or according to packet instructions until 'al dente'.

To make the pesto, place the semi sun-dried tomatoes in a food processor or liquidiser with the garlic and basil leaves and pulse to finely chop. Switch the machine back on and slowly pour in the oil through the feeder tube until the pesto has emulsified. Transfer to a bowl with a spatula and season to taste. This can be made up to 3-4 days in advance and kept covered with clingfilm in the fridge.

Drain the pasta, quickly refresh and then return to the pan. Add the roasted aubergine mixture, lemon rind and juice, stirring to combine. Finally fold in the basil and enough of the pesto to coat - use any remaining in other dishes. Season to taste.

To Serve Tip the pasta into a warmed serving bowls and scatter over the Gruyère. Garnish with the basil sprigs and place straight on the table so that people can help themselves into warmed serving bowls.

Tip If you aren't really sure what 'al dente' really means there is another way that the Italians check to see if their pasta is cooked. They throw a piece against the wall and if it sticks, it's ready to eat! I'm just not so sure that this would go down too well in Ireland . . .

Smoked Bacon and Tomato Pizza Bread

Serves 6-8

This Italian flat bread is really easy to make and will taste so much better than any of the shop-bought focaccia-style breads which can be hard to find and are normally very expensive. You can vary the toppings, but be careful to go light on them, so as not to load down the tasty base.

Ingredients

12oz / 350g strong plain bread flour, plus extra for dusting
2 teaspoons fast action dried yeast (7g sachet)
1 tablespoon olive oil, plus extra for greasing
4fl oz / 120ml tepid milk
1/4 pint / 150ml tepid water

For the Tomato Sauce

1 tablespoon olive oil
4 tomatoes, roughly chopped
2 garlic cloves, crushed
14fl oz / 400ml passata (sieved tomatoes)
2 tablespoons tomato puree
2 tablespoons torn fresh basil

For the Topping

8 smoked streaky bacon rashers
1 red onion, thinly sliced into rings
2oz / 50g Cheddar, finely grated
4 tablespoons homemade basil pesto (see tip) or shop-bought
salt and freshly ground black pepper

Method Sieve the flour into a large bowl with one teaspoon of salt and stir in the dried yeast. Make a well in the centre and pour the oil, tepid milk and water in and mix to a smooth dough. Turn out on to a lightly floured surface and knead for 5-10 minutes, pushing and stretching the dough until smooth and elastic. Alternatively use a food mixer with the dough hook attached and set on a low speed - it saves quite a bit of elbow grease.

Place the dough in a large, lightly oiled bowl. Cover with a clean cloth and leave in a warm place for 1 hour until the dough has almost doubled in size.

Meanwhile, make the tomato sauce. Heat the oil in a sauté pan and cook the fresh tomatoes and garlic for 4-5 minutes, until softened and pulpy, stirring occasionally. Add the passata, tomato puree and basil and simmer for about 45 minutes until the sauce has reduced and thickened. Season to taste and leave to cool.

Knock the risen dough back punching it lightly to knock out large air bubbles and knead briefly on a lightly floured surface. Roll out the dough to fit a 15in x 11in / 37.5cm x 27.5cm baking tray (Swiss roll tin). Transfer the dough into the tray with a rolling pin and gently press in the edges to fit up the sides. Spread the tomato sauce over the dough, leaving a 1/2 in / 1cm border around the edge. Sprinkle the onion on top and then scatter over the Cheddar. Cover with a tea towel and leave to rise for another 30 minutes.

Preheat the oven to 200C/400F/Gas 6. Bake the pizza bread for 15-20 minutes until bubbling and golden. Preheat the grill to medium. Arrange the bacon rashers on a grill rack and grill for a few minutes each side until crisp and golden. Drain on kitchen paper and then chop into pieces.

To Serve Loosen the pizza bread from the baking tray and slide out on to a chopping board. Sprinkle over the chopped bacon and drizzle the pesto on top, then cut into slices. Pile into a bread basket for the table.

Tip To make pesto, place two handfuls of basil leaves in a food processor with two peeled garlic cloves, a couple of tablespoons of toasted pine nuts and pour in enough olive oil to make a smooth puree. Season to taste. Store in a jar in the fridge.

Wheaten Bread

Makes 2 x 1 1/2 pint / 900ml loaves

The smell of freshly baked wheaten bread always reminds me of my Granny's house. She's always baking loaves of wheaten bread and says that speed is the key to success: they should be mixed in seconds and really ought to be eaten within hours. We always bake it in the restaurant first thing in the morning for guests that have stayed overnight so that the smell is wafting around the house as they wake up. Not surprisingly, it always seems to go down a treat.

Ingredients

1lb / 450g plain flour, plus extra for dusting
1 1/2 teaspoons bicarbonate of soda
large pinch salt
4oz / 100g butter, plus extra for greasing
4oz / 100g bran flakes
1 tablespoon light muscovado sugar
2 tablespoons golden syrup
1 1/2 pints / 900ml buttermilk
butter for spreading, to serve

Method Preheat oven to 200C/400F/Gas 6.

Sieve the flour into a bowl with the bicarbonate of soda and salt. Rub in the butter with your fingertips until evenly dispersed.

Stir in the bran and muscovado sugar and then make a well in the centre and add the golden syrup and buttermilk. Using a large spoon, mix gently and quickly until you have achieved a nice dropping consistency.

Pour into 2 x 1 1/2 pint / 900ml greased tins with the bases lined with a rectangle of parchment paper and bake for 45 minutes to 1 hour or until the loaves are golden and have cracked slightly on top. To check, tip the loaf out of the tin and tap the base. It should sound hollow. If it doesn't return it to the oven for another 5 minutes. Tip out on to a wire rack and when cool enough to handle carefully peel off the parchment paper. Leave to cool completely.

To Serve Place the wheaten bread on a breadboard and cut into slices at the table. Hand around with a separate pot of butter for spreading.

Tip This wheaten bread is also delicious sprinkled with a couple of tablespoons of sesame seeds or sunflower seeds before baking.

Cheese and Onion Bread

Makes 1 x 2 pint/1.2 litre loaf

Fresh yeast can be hard to find which is why I've given you the option of using dried. However, most bakers still use the fresh variety as it gives a better flavour so try blagging some from your local bakery and freeze any leftover. I normally use Dubliner Cheddar cheese to make this bread that has a mild, tangy flavour.

Ingredients
3oz / 75g butter, plus extra for greasing
1 onion, finely chopped
1oz / 25g fresh yeast or 1 tablespoon fast action dried yeast
pinch caster sugar
½ pint / 300ml lukewarm water
1lb / 450g strong plain flour, plus extra for dusting
1 teaspoon salt
1 teaspoon wholegrain mustard
4oz / 100g Cheddar cheese, finely grated
butter for spreading, to serve

Method Melt 1oz / 25g of the butter in a frying pan and sauté the onion for about 10 minutes until it is soft and light golden. Remove from the heat and leave to cool.

Dissolve the fresh yeast, if using, and sugar in a little of the warm water. Place the flour in bowl with the salt and dried yeast, if using. Stir in the water, yeast mix and sugar, if using. Mix in the sautéed onion, mustard and half of the Cheddar until you have achieved a slightly, sticky dough.

Turn the dough out on to a lightly floured surface and knead for 5-10 minutes, pushing and stretching the dough until smooth and elastic. Alternatively use a food mixer with the dough hook attached and set on a low speed - it saves quite a bit of elbow grease. Place the dough in a large, lightly greased bowl. Cover with a clean cloth and leave in a warm place for about 1 hour or until the dough has doubled in size.

Melt the remaining butter in a small pan or in the microwave. Allow to cool a little. Knock the risen dough back punching it lightly to knock out large air bubbles and knead gently on a lightly floured surface until smooth. Divide into 20 small balls and then shape into rounds.

Place half of rounds into a 2 pint / 1.2 litre loaf tin and brush with some of melted butter. Cover with the rest of the rounds and brush with the remaining melted butter. Sprinkle the rest of the grated Cheese on top and cover with a tea towel. Set aside in a warm place for 1 hour or until doubled in size.

Preheat the oven to 190C/375F/Gas 5. Bake the loaf for 40-45 minutes or until well risen and golden brown. Test that the loaf is cooked by tapping on the base - it should sound hallow. If not give it another 5 minutes and test again. Transfer to a wire rack and leave to cool slightly.

To Serve Place the cheese and onion bread in a bread basket. Hand around with the butter.

● **Tip** Rising times for dough should always only be used as a guide, but generally speaking 1 hour in a warm place is about right. Otherwise, it can take up to 2 hours at room temperature or overnight in the fridge.

Gluten-Free Bread

Makes 1 loaf

There has always been a tremendous response when I've cooked gluten-free recipes on *Open House* and over the years many viewers who are coeliacs have written to me looking for a good gluten-free white yeast bread recipe, as it can be very difficult to find tasty shop-bought loaves. The bread has a completely different texture to ordinary bread. It is a much lighter mix and sinks back into the tin slightly as it is cooling, so don't think you have done anything wrong!

Ingredients
140z / 400g gluten-free flour, plus extra for dusting
2 teaspoons fast action dried yeast (7g sachet)
1/2 teaspoon salt
2oz / 50g milk powder
1 tablespoon Xanthan gum
2 teaspoons caster sugar
3/4 pint / 450ml lukewarm water
2 eggs, beaten
4 tablespoons sunflower oil, plus extra for greasing
1 tablespoon sesame seeds
butter for spreading, to serve

Method Sift the flour into a large bowl with the yeast, salt, milk powder, Xanthan gum and sugar. Make a well in the centre and add the water, eggs and oil. Using a wooden spoon, mix together until it forms a soft moist mixture and then beat for 1 minute until well combined.

Spoon the mixture into a 2 pint / 1.2 litre lightly oiled loaf tin and smooth the surface, using slightly wetted hands. Sprinkle over the sesame seeds and cover with a tea towel. Leave to rise in a warm place for about 1 hour or until the loaf has risen to the top of the tin.

Preheat the oven to 190C/375F/Gas 5. Bake the bread for 40-45 minutes or until golden brown. Test that the loaf is cooked by tapping on the base - it should sound hollow, if not give it another 5 minutes and test again. Leave in the tin for 5 minutes and then transfer to a wire rack and allow to cool completely.

To Serve Place the bread on a breadboard while it is still warm and cut into slices at the table. Hand around with a separate pot of butter for spreading.

Tip Gluten-free flour and Xanthan gum are available from good health food shops and some large chemists. There are also a number of companies offering good mail-order services via the Internet.

Vanilla and Crème Brûlée with Poached Plums

Serves 6

I normally use a blowtorch for this recipe, but you do need to be careful with them and they are definitely not for the faint-hearted. Alternatively, place the brûlées under a hot grill, but watch them like a hawk because they do burn very easily. When glazed they should be a nice mahogany brown colour.

Ingredients
8 egg yolks
9oz / 250g caster sugar
1 vanilla pod, split and seeds scraped out
½ pint / 300ml milk
1 pint / 600ml cream
14oz / 400g can coconut milk

For the Plums
¼ pint / 150ml red wine
1 cinnamon stick
1 whole star anise
1 vanilla pod, split and seeds scraped out
1lb / 450g ripe plums, halved and stoned
1 teaspoon finely grated fresh root ginger
175g / 6oz caster sugar
fresh mint leaves, to decorate
vanilla ice cream, to serve (good quality)

Method Preheat oven to 90C/185F/Gas 1/4. Place the egg yolks in a large bowl with 4½oz / 125g of the sugar and the scraped out vanilla seeds. Whisk for about 5 minutes until pale and fluffy, and the mixture will hold a trail of the figure eight.

Meanwhile, place the milk in a pan with the cream, coconut milk and scraped out vanilla pod and then simmer gently until the mixture just comes to the boil. Slowly pour the hot coconut milk into the yolk mixture, whisking continuously. Pass through a sieve into a clean bowl.

Using a ladle, divide the mixture into 6 x 7fl oz / 200ml ramekins set on a baking sheet. Bake in the oven for 30-40 minutes or until just set but still with a slight wobble in the middle, then switch off the oven and leave to cool. Transfer to the fridge and allow to set for at least 6 hours, or preferably overnight.

To poach the plums, place the wine in a pan with ¼ pint / 150ml of water, the sugar, cinnamon, star anise and scraped out vanilla seeds and then bring to the boil. Reduce the heat and simmer gently for 20-25 minutes until reduced by half and syrupy in texture. Transfer to a bowl, cover with clingfilm and chill until needed.

Add the plums and ginger to the reduced down wine mixture and simmer for another 4-5 minutes until softened but still holding their shape, stirring occasionally but being careful not to damage the plums. Remove from the heat and leave to cool completely.

To Serve Sprinkle the brûlées in an even layer with the remaining caster sugar and then use a blowtorch to melt and glaze the sugar until caramelised. Arrange on serving plates and spoon on poached plums with a little of their syrup. Decorate with the mint leaves and add a scoop of ice cream to each plate.

Tip Use the best quality Bourbon vanilla pods. They can be used again to make vanilla sugar; just rinse and dry them as necessary before pushing them into a bag of sugar. Leave for two weeks. It's as simple as that.

Exotic Panna Cotta with Strawberry Coulis

Serves 6

Panna cotta is a set Italian cream that is almost a cross between a crème brûlée (without the crunchy topping) and a mousse. What makes them so special is the addition of the coconut milk, giving them a truly exotic flavour. They really do look stunning with the swirls of strawberry coulis and decorated with whole strawberries and mint sprigs. I'm getting a bit carried away with the prose, but this dessert really is a stylish way to end a meal.

Ingredients
4 gelatine leaves (a scant 15g / ½oz)
1 vanilla pod, split and seeds scraped out
17fl oz / 500ml cream
3 ½fl oz / 100ml coconut milk
4oz / 100g caster sugar

For the Strawberry Coulis
7oz / 200g fresh strawberries, hulled
2oz / 50g caster sugar
whole strawberries and fresh small mint leaves, to decorate

Method To make the panna cotta, put the gelatine leaves into a bowl of cold water and leave them to soak for 10 minutes. Put the cream, coconut milk, caster sugar and scraped out vanilla seeds into a pan and slowly bring up to the boil. Take the pan off the heat, gently squeeze the soaked gelatine leaves dry and add, whisking continuously until they have dissolved. Strain the mixture through a sieve into a measuring jug.

Divide the mixture equally between 6 x ¼ pint / 150ml dariole moulds or ramekins, place them on a baking tray and leave them to set in fridge for at least 3 hours or up to two days is fine.

Meanwhile make the strawberry coulis. Briefly blend the strawberry and caster sugar in a food processor or liquidiser until smooth. Press through a fine sieve into a small bowl to remove all the seeds. Cover with clingfilm and chill until needed.

To Serve Unmould the panna cotta by dipping them briefly into hot water and arrange on serving plates. Drizzle over a little of the strawberry coulis and decorate each plate with a few extra strawberries and the mint leaves.

Tip The easiest way to slit open the vanilla pods lengthways is with the tip of a small sharp knife and then use it or a teaspoon to scrape out the seeds.

Chocolate Mousse with Orange Caramel Sauce

Serves 6

These mousses are perfectly decadent with just the perfect hint of Baileys - delicious! For such a simple dessert, it really will impress and you can have it prepared well in advance with no last minute worries. There is definitely something romantic about chocolate and this tasty mousse will have your partner swooning in their seat. The orange caramel sauce cuts through the richness of the chocolate mousse.

Ingredients
8oz / 225g plain chocolate (at least 50% cocoa solids)
3 eggs
1 tablesooon Baileys Irish cream
1/2 pint / 300ml cream

For the Orange Caramel Sauce
8oz / 225g caster sugar
1/2 pint / 300ml freshly squeezed orange juice
lightly whipped cream, whole raspberries and chocolate flakes, to decorate

Method Break the chocolate into squares and place in a heatproof bowl set over a pan of simmering water until melted. Remove from the heat and leave to cool.

Whisk the eggs with the Baileys in a separate heatproof bowl over the pan of simmering water until it has doubled in size. It is very important to make sure that the water does not boil or you will be in danger of cooking the eggs.

Whisk the cream in a bowl until it is just holding its shape. Fold the melted chocolate into the egg mixture and allow to cool for 5 minutes, then fold in the whipped cream until well combined. Divide the mixture among pretty serving glasses, not quite filling each one right up to the top and chill for at least 2-3 hours or overnight is best.

To make the orange caramel sauce, place the sugar in a heavy-based pan with 1/4 pint / 150ml of cold water and cook until the sugar has dissolved, then simmer gently until you have achieved golden caramel, without stirring. This should take about 15 minutes in total.

Strain the orange juice into the pan through a fine sieve and cook for another 2 minutes, stirring to combine with a wooden spoon. It will splutter and create plenty of steam so be careful. Remove from the heat and leave to cool, then pour into a jug and chill until needed. This will keep well in the fridge for 2-3 days.

To Serve Drizzle a little of the orange caramel sauce over the mousses and place the remainder on the table so that people can help themselves. Decorate each mousse with the lightly whipped cream, raspberries and chocolate flakes.

Tip The higher the percentage of cocoa in the chocolate you use, the better the mousses will taste and also the less sugar that will be present.

Apple and Almond Tart

Serves 6

The best way to arrange the apples in the tin is to start at the perimeter, in a pinwheel fashion, filling the middle after a full circle of slices is in place. It is important that they are tightly packed and pressed down gently into the filling or they are in danger of 'springing' during the cooking process.

Ingredients
5oz / 150g butter
100g/4oz icing sugar, sifted
1oz / 25g plain flour
4oz / 100g ground almonds
2 eggs, lightly beaten
1 vanilla pod, split and seeds scraped out
large pinch ground cinnamon
1lb / 450g cooking apples
juice of 1/2 lemon
2-3 tablespoons apricot jam

For the Pastry
4oz / 100g butter, diced
6oz / 175g plain flour, plus extra for dusting
pinch salt
2oz / 50g caster sugar
1 egg yolk
1/2 tablespoon cream
softly whipped cream and caramel ice cream, to serve

Method To make the pastry, place the butter in a food processor with the flour, salt and sugar and pulse until just blended. Add the egg yolk and cream and blend again briefly. Be careful not to overwork or the pastry will be tough. Cover with clingfilm and chill for 1 hour to rest.

To make the filling, place 4oz / 100g of the butter and the icing sugar in a large bowl and beat until light and fluffy, using an electric hand beater. Beat in the flour and almonds and then gradually beat in the eggs, scraped out vanilla seeds and cinnamon. Continue to beat for 5 minutes until light and fluffy.

Preheat oven to 190C/375F/Gas 5. Roll out the pastry on a lightly floured surface and use to line a 9in / 23cm loose-bottomed flan tin. Chill again for 15 minutes to allow the pastry to rest.

Peel the apples and cut into quarters to remove the cores, then cut into thin wedges. Tip into a bowl and toss in the lemon juice to prevent them from browning. Spread the almond filling in the pastry case and carefully arrange the apple slices on top in a fan shape and then gently press the apples down into the filling. Dot with the remaining 1oz / 25g of the butter.

Bake the tart for 25-30 minutes until the pastry is cooked through and the apples are golden brown. Remove from the flan tin and transfer to a plate. Melt the apricot jam in a small pan or in the microwave and brush over the tart.

To Serve Cut the tart into wedges and serve warm or cold on serving plates with a good dollop of whipped cream and a scoop of caramel ice cream.

Tip Once the pastry has rested, roll it out about 2in / 5cm larger than the tin, then use a rolling pin to help you lift the pastry over the tin. Lift the edges of the pastry so that they fall down into the tin, then gently press against the edges trimming with a sharp knife: it's that simple!

Mango and Gingernut Cheesecake

Serves 8

This cheesecake combines a luscious tropical fruit topping with a creamy filling and a spiced biscuit base. I think that gelatine leaves are much easier to use than powdered gelatine. They are available from good delis. Otherwise use two teaspoons for the filling and dissolve in two tablespoons of very hot water and use one teaspoon for the topping and dissolve in one tablespoon of very hot water.

Ingredients
4oz / 100g butter
7oz / 200g gingernut biscuits
vegetable oil, for greasing

For the Filling
4 gelatine leaves (a scant 1/2oz / 15g)
6fl oz / 175ml milk
1 vanilla pod, split and seeds scraped out
6oz / 175g caster sugar
17fl oz / 500ml thick Greek yoghurt
finely grated rind and juice of 2 limes
1/4 pint / 150ml cream

For the Topping
2 gelatine leaves (a scant 1/4oz / 10g)
14oz / 400g can mango slices in syrup, drained
strawberry coulis (page 91), to serve
fresh mint leaves, to decorate

Method To make the base, melt the butter in a small pan or in the microwave. Place the biscuits in a food processor or liquidiser and blend to fine crumbs. With the motor still running, pour in the melted butter through the feeder tube and mix until well combined. Tip into a lightly oiled 9in / 23cm loose-bottomed cake tin and press firmly and evenly to form a base for the cheesecake. Chill for at least 10 minutes until firmly set or up to 24 hours is fine.

Meanwhile, make the filling. Soak the gelatine leaves in a bowl of cold water for 10 minutes. Place the milk in a pan and add the scraped out vanilla seeds, whisking to combine. Cook until it just reaches boiling point, but do not allow to boil. Gently squeeze the gelatine dry and add to the pan with the sugar, whisking until dissolved. Pour into a large bowl and leave to cool a little.

Stir the Greek yoghurt into the cooled milk mixture with the lime rind and juice. Whip the cream in a separate bowl until it is just holding its shape, then fold into the filling mixture. Pour into the set biscuit base and chill for at least 1 hour until set or up to 24 hours is fine.

To make the topping, soak the gelatine leaves in a bowl of cold water for 10 minutes. Place the mango slices in a mini processor or liquidiser and blend until smooth. Heat one tablespoon of water in a small saucepan or in the microwave. Gently squeeze the gelatine dry and stir into the hot water until dissolved. Add to the mango puree and pour over the set cheesecake filling, spreading evenly with the back of a spoon. Chill for another 2-3 hours until completely set or up to 24 hours is fine.

To Serve Remove the cheesecake from the tin and transfer to a serving plate. Cut into slices and arrange on individual serving plates with a swirl of the strawberry coulis. Decorate with the mint leaves.

Tip Replace the can of mangoes with a can of peaches or apricots for the same lovely contrast of colours.

Roast Pineapple with Coconut Rice Pudding

Serves 6

Rice pudding is excellent comfort food and I'm sure on most people's lists of favourite childhood desserts. If you are short of time, you can microwave the rice pudding, although you won't get the same depth of flavour.

Ingredients
1 small fresh pineapple, peeled, cored and cut into wedges
8oz / 225g caster sugar
1/4 pint / 150ml pineapple juice
1/2 vanilla pod, split and seeds scraped out

For the Rice Pudding
1/2 pint / 300ml milk
7fl oz / 200ml cream
4oz / 100g short grain pudding rice
1oz / 25g butter
3oz / 75g caster sugar
finely grated rind of 1 orange
14oz / 400g can coconut milk
1/2 vanilla pod, split

Method Preheat the oven to 150c/300F/Gas 2.

To make the caramel pineapple sauce, place the sugar in a small heavy-based pan with 1/4 pint / 150ml cold water and cook until the sugar has dissolved, then simmer gently until you have achieved a golden caramel, without stirring. This should take no more than 15 minutes in total.

Stir the pineapple juice into the caramel with the scraped out vanilla seeds and cook for another 2 minutes, stirring to combine with a wooden spoon. It will splutter and create plenty of steam so be careful. Remove from the heat and leave to cool. Then pour into a jug and chill until needed. This will keep in the fridge for 2-3 days.

Arrange the pineapple wedges in a baking tray and drizzle over three tablespoons of the pineapple caramel sauce, then stir until well coated. Roast for 15-20 minutes or until the pineapple is roasted and lightly golden, tossing the tray occasionally to prevent it from catching and burning - if in doubt drizzle around a tablespoon of water.

To make the rice pudding, place the milk in a pan with the cream and bring to a simmer. Stir in the rice, butter, sugar, orange rind, vanilla pod and coconut milk and bring to the boil, stirring until the sugar has dissolved. Reduce the heat to the lowest setting and cook for 45 minutes or until the rice is tender and creamy, stirring frequently. Remove the vanilla pod from the pan.

To Serve Spoon the roasted pineapple wedges into the centre of warmed serving plates. Spoon the rice pudding to one side and then drizzle around the remaining caramel sauce.

Tip To check that a pineapple is ripe, give it a good sniff - it should smell fragrant, and then try to gently pull out one of the centre leaves - if it comes away easily then you'll know that the pineapple is definitely ripe.

Warm Chocolate Brownie with Fudge Sauce

Serves 6-8

There is definitely something about chocolate that is addictive. It contains several stimulants, including caffeine and pleasure-inducing endorphins! These are intensely chocolaty brownies that get smothered in a rich fudge sauce that is flavoured with - you've guessed it, more chocolate! Beware of nut allergies when serving these to children - if in doubt - check!

Ingredients
14oz / 400g plain chocolate, finely chopped (at least 70% cocoa solids)
8oz / 225g butter
4 eggs
10oz / 300g caster sugar
4oz / 100g self-raising flour
3oz / 75g cocoa powder
4oz / 100g mixed nuts, roughly chopped

For the Fudge Sauce
½ pint / 300ml cream
3oz / 75g caster sugar
2oz / 50g butter
12oz / 350g plain chocolate, finely chopped (at least 70% cocoa solids)
vanilla ice cream, to serve

Method Preheat the oven to 170C/325F/Gas 3.

Place 4oz / 100g of the chocolate in a heatproof bowl with the butter and set over a pan of simmering water until melted, then stir to combine. Remove from the heat and leave to cool a little.

Meanwhile, whisk the eggs in a bowl until stiff and holding their shape, then whisk in the sugar until you have achieved a stiff sabayon that can hold a trail of the figure eight. Sift the flour and cocoa powder into the sabayon and lightly fold in. Add the melted chocolate mixture with the remaining 10oz / 300g of finely chopped chocolate and the nuts and continue folding gently until all the ingredients are just combined.

Pour the chocolate mixture into a deep-sided baking tin that is about 11in x 7in / 27.5cm x 18cm and has been lined with parchment paper. Bake for 35-40 minutes until the top is crusty but the centre is still a little soft.

Meanwhile, make the fudge sauce. Place the cream in a pan with the sugar and butter and bring to the boil, stirring. Reduce the heat and simmer gently for a few minutes until thickened and toffee-like, stirring occasionally to prevent the mixture from sticking. Remove from heat and leave to cool.

Place the chocolate for the sauce in a heatproof bowl set over a pan of simmering water until melted. Whisk into the sauce until smooth and well combined. Leave to cool completely, then transfer to a bowl, cover with clingfilm and keep in the fridge until needed. It should keep happily for up to 1 week.

To Serve Remove brownies from the oven and allow to cool in the tin for about 5 minutes, then remove from the tin and peel off the parchment paper. Transfer the fudge sauce to a pan and gently heat through, or pierce the clingfim and heat in the microwave. Cut the brownies into rectangles and arrange on serving plates with the hot fudge sauce and scoops of the ice cream.

Tip If the brownies have gone cold and you want to heat them up in a hurry, pour over some of the fudge sauce and flash under a hot grill until bubbling.

Poached Pears with Meringue

Serves 4

A combination of pears and light crisp meringue surrounded with a spiced syrup will revive even the most jaded palate, so put some spice in your life! However, spices do not last indefinitely and if they've been hanging around too long you might as well be using sawdust. The best thing to do is to always give them a good sniff to check their flavour; if they are not strongly scented, they have lost their taste, too.

Ingredients
1 pint / 600ml apple juice
1 cinnamon stick
½ vanilla pod, split
2 whole star anise
4oz / 100g caster sugar
4 firm, ripe pears (Conference, if possible)
1 orange, cut into slices

For the Meringue
2 egg whites
4oz / 100g caster sugar
½ vanilla pod, split and seeds scraped out
1 tablespoon toasted flaked almonds
vanilla ice cream, to serve
fresh mint sprigs, to decorate

Method Place the apple juice in a pan with the cinnamon stick, vanilla pod, star anise and caster sugar. Cook gently until the sugar has dissolved, stirring occasionally.

Peel the pears, cut each one in half and then scoop out the cores with a teaspoon. Add to the apple juice mixture with the orange slices and bring to the boil, then reduce the heat and simmer for 15-20 minutes until tender. Remove from the heat and leave the pears to cool completely in the poaching liquid.

Transfer the pears on to a plate with a slotted spoon, reserving the poaching liquid. Return the poaching liquid to the heat and simmer gently for 10-15 minutes until reduced to a syrup. Leave to cool, then strain into a jug. Cover with clingfilm and chill until needed. This will keep happily in the fridge for 2 to 3 days.

Preheat oven to 190C/375F/Gas 5. To make the meringue, whisk the egg whites in a bowl until stiff. Add the scraped out vanilla seeds and then gradually whisk in the sugar, a tablespoon at a time, until the meringue holds its shape and is shiny and glossy.

Arrange the pears in a baking tray and spoon enough of the meringue on top of each one to cover, using a tablespoon. Bake for 5 minutes or until meringue is golden. Pour the reserved spiced syrup into a small pan and heat through gently, or use the microwave - just remember to pierce the clingfilm.

To Serve Arrange pear halves on serving plates and drizzle around the spiced syrup. The remaining syrup doesn't have to go to waste and is lovely in a fresh fruit salad. Sprinkle the flaked almonds over the poached pears with meringue and add a scoop of ice cream to each one. Decorate with the mint sprigs.

Tip It is crucial that the pears are covered completely with liquid while they are being poached. Add a little extra boiling water to the pan if you are worried, or just take the easy option and use a can of pear halves in syrup.

Roast Turkey with Sage, Apricot and Pine Nut Stuffing

Serves 10-12

To ensure your turkey is properly cooked, insert a fine skewer into the thickest part of the thigh - the juices should run clear. If they are still pink, return to the oven and check again every 15 minutes. Allow 20 minutes per 1lb / 450g plus 20 minutes extra - this size turkey should take about 4 hours and 20 minutes.

Ingredients

12lb / 6kg oven-ready turkey, at room temperature (preferably free-range)
4oz / 100g butter, at room temperature
4 rindless streaky bacon rashers
5oz / 150g pitted prunes (ready-to-eat)
1lb / 450g cocktail sausages
1 tablespoon plain flour
3 tablespoons ruby red port or red wine
1 pint / 600ml turkey stock

For Sage, Onion and Pine Nut Stuffing

2oz / 50g pine nuts
3oz / 75g butter
1 large onion, diced
6oz / 175g fresh white breadcrumbs
1 tablespoon chopped fresh parsley
1 teaspoon chopped fresh sage
4 ready-to-eat dried apricots, finely chopped
salt and freshly ground black pepper
Crispy roast potatoes with thyme and garlic (page 113), Roast root vegetables with honey and parsley (page 111) and Brussels sprouts with bacon (page 112)
small bunch fresh herbs, to garnish (to include parsley, sage and bay leaves)

Method Preheat the oven to 190C/375F/Gas 5. To make the stuffing, heat a frying pan. Add the pine nuts and cook until toasted, tossing occasionally. Tip into a bowl. Melt the butter in the same pan and add onion, then cook for a few minutes until softened but not coloured. Place the breadcrumbs in a bowl and add the toasted pine nuts, onion and butter mixture, parsley, sage and apricots. Mix well to combine and season to taste. To stuff the turkey, gently loosen the neck flap away from the breast and you'll be able to make a triangular pocket. Pack in the stuffing and make a neat round shape on the outside, then tuck the neck flap underneath and secure it with a small skewer.

Cut bacon into strips and use to wrap prunes. Put on a plate with the sausages, cover with clingfilm and chill. Smear the skin of the turkey all over with some of the butter and season. Turn the turkey breast-side up and tie the top of the drumsticks with string. Weigh to calculate the required cooking time. Lay a large sheet of foil lengthways over a large roasting tin, leaving enough at each end to wrap over the turkey, then lightly butter the foil. Repeat this with another sheet of foil, this time across the tin. Lightly butter once again. Place the turkey breast-side up in the centre of the foil, then wrap loosely to enclose.

Place in the oven and cook according to your calculated cooking time, carefully unwrapping and baste every 40 minutes. For the final hour, fold back and remove the foil, baste well and return to the oven. Add the bacon wrapped prunes and cocktail sausages for the last 30 minutes and allow to finish cooking. The turkey should be a rich, dark brown colour. Remove from the oven and transfer to a serving platter, surround with the bacon wrapped prunes and cocktail sausages. Cover with foil and leave to rest in a warm place.

Place the roasting tin on the hob over a gentle heat and skim any excess fat from the cooking juices. Stir the flour into the tin's residue. Cook on the hob for 1-2 minutes, stirring until golden. Pour in the port or red wine, stirring to combine, then gradually add the stock, stirring until smooth after each addition. Bring to the boil and let it bubble for about 10 minutes until reduced and thickened, stirring. Season to taste.

To Serve Garnish the turkey with the bunch of herbs. Carve into slices and arrange on warmed serving plates with some of the gravy, the roast potatoes, vegetables and all of the trimmings.

Irish Whiskey and Maple Glazed Ham

Serves 10-12

A traditional ham is the perfect choice if you've got hoards of visitors to feed. It's especially good to have over the festive period. A certain crowd pleaser, it tastes equally good served hot or cold. Have you ever wondered what the difference is between ham, bacon and gammon? Bacon is cured pork; gammon is a hind leg cut of bacon; and once this particular cut is cooked, it is called ham. Bet you are not confused now . . .

Ingredients
11lb / 5.25kg leg of gammon (on the bone)
4 celery sticks, roughly chopped
2 onions, sliced
1 bunch fresh thyme
1 tablespoon black peppercorns
7fl oz / 200ml Irish whiskey
7fl oz / 200ml maple syrup
3 teaspoons ground allspice
1 teaspoon whole cloves

Method Although gammon is less salty nowadays, soaking is still a good idea. Place the gammon in a large pan and cover with cold water. Leave to soak for at least 6 hours or overnight is best, then drain.

Weigh the gammon joint and calculate the cooking time, allowing 20 minutes per 1lb / 450g plus 20 minutes - this joint should take about 4 hours. Place in a large pan and cover with water and bring to the boil, skimming off any scum. Add the celery, onion, thyme and peppercorns and return to the boil. Then cover, reduce the heat and simmer until completely tender, occasionally skimming off any scum that rises to the top, topping up with water as necessary. If you are not sure about whether the gammon is properly cooked check the bone end - it should come away freely from the gammon joint. Drain and leave until cool enough to handle.

Preheat the oven to 180C/350F/Gas 4. Carefully peel away the skin, leaving the layer of white fat intact. Using a sharp knife, score the fat diagonally to make a diamond pattern, being careful not to cut into the meat. Place the whiskey in a pan with the maple syrup and ground allspice. Bring to the boil and simmer for about 10 minutes until slightly thickened. Stud the ham with the cloves and place in a large roasting tin with a little water to prevent the bottom from sticking and burning. Brush the syrup all over the ham. Cook for 1 hour, basting every 15 minutes to ensure an even glaze. Remove the cooked ham from the oven, transfer to a serving platter and leave to rest for 15 minutes.

To Serve Carve slices from one side of the ham, cutting diagonally to achieve an even thickness. When you reach the bone, insert the knife at a flatter angle and slice across the top of the bone. Turn over the leg to carve slices from the other sides.

Tip Any leftovers from this ham or your turkey can be used in countless other dishes, such as in a creamy filling for vol-au-vents, in risottos or the ham is excellent for a spaghetti carbonara. There's no waste - even the bone will make a wonderful stock.

Roast Goose with Apple and Cranberry Stuffing

Serves 8

There was a time when goose, rather than turkey, was the traditional family treat at Christmas. Thankfully in the last few years it has come back into its own and supplies of free-range birds are now plentiful during the festive period. It is what we'd always have as a family at Christmas, served with all of the trimmings. Save the drained off fat and use to make my crispy roast potatoes with thyme and garlic (page 113).

Ingredients
12lb / 6kg oven-ready goose
1 teaspoon salt
2 tablespoons redcurrant jelly
1 tablespoon ruby red port or red wine
finely grated rind of 1 orange
2 eating apples, peeled, cored and cut into wedges
4oz / 100g fresh cranberries
24 asparagus spears, peeled

For the Apple and Cranberry Stuffing
2 tablespoons olive oil
2 eating apples, peeled, cored and cut into thin slices
1 tablespoon chopped fresh thyme
12oz / 350g sausage meat (good quality)
3oz / 75g fresh white breadcrumbs
4oz / 100g dried cranberries
4oz /100g walnut halves, chopped
salt and freshly ground black pepper
Crispy roast potatoes with thyme and garlic (page 113), Roast root vegetables with honey and parsley (page 111) Brussels sprouts with bacon (page 112)
small bunch fresh thyme sprigs, to garnish

Method To make the stuffing, heat the oil in a large frying pan. Add the apples and sauté for 3-4 minutes until softened and golden. Transfer to a bowl and leave to cool. Add the thyme, sausage meat, breadcrumbs, cranberries and walnuts, stirring gently until evenly mixed. Season to taste.

Preheat oven to 200C/400F/Gas 6. Place the goose on a rack set over a roasting tin. Pour over a kettle of boiling water, then drain off the water from the roasting tin. To stuff the goose, start at the neck end where you'll find a flap of loose skin: gently loosen this away from the breast and you'll be able to make a triangular pocket. Pack in two-thirds of the stuffing inside and make a neat round shape on the outside, then tuck the neck flap under the goose and secure it with a small skewer. Rub all over with salt.

Press the remaining stuffing into the base of 1lb / 450g loaf tin and set aside. Weigh the goose and calculate the cooking time, allowing 15 minutes per 1lb / 450g plus 15 minutes - this goose should take about 3 1/2 hours. Place in the oven to roast, draining off excess fat every 30 minutes or so and after 1 hour reduce the oven temperature to 180C/350F/Gas 4. Continue to cook, still draining the fat off every 30 minutes.

Remove the goose from the oven 30 minutes before the end of the cooking time. Drain off all but 2 tablespoons of the fat and add the apple wedges, cranberries and asparagus, tossing to coat. Warm the redcurrant jelly in a small pan or in the microwave and stir in the port or wine with the orange rind, then brush over the goose. Return the goose to the oven with the reserved tin of extra stuffing and cook for the final 30 minutes until completely tender. Transfer the goose to a serving platter and cover with foil. Then leave to rest for 10 minutes. Place the cranberry, apple and asparagus mixture into a warmed serving bowl.

To Serve Garnish the roast goose with thyme and bring to the table. Turn the tin of extra stuffing on to a warmed serving plate. Carve into slices and arrange on warmed serving plates with some of the stuffing, roasted cranberries, apples and asparagus, the potatoes and vegetables.

Tip Pouring the kettle of boiling water over the goose shrinks the skin and helps to remove excess fat.

Roasted Root Vegetables with Honey and Parsley

Serves 8-10

Roasting is a great way to cook root vegetables as they're robust enough to cope with the intense heat, and the honey helps draw out the most wonderful flavours. This recipe also makes life much easier on Christmas day as all the preparation can be done well in advance so there's really nothing to them. Just make sure that all your vegetables are roughly the same size to ensure even cooking. Any leftovers can be blitzed with stock for an instant soup.

Ingredients
3 tablespoons olive oil
3lb / 1.5kg carrots, trimmed and halved lengthways
3lb / 1.5kg large parsnips, trimmed, quartered and cored
3 tablespoons clear honey
1 teaspoon toasted sesame seeds
3 tablespoons chopped fresh parsley
Salt and freshly ground black pepper

Method Preheat the oven to 180C/350F/Gas 4.

Place the oil in a large roasting tin and add the carrots and parsnips, tossing until well coated. Season generously. Roast for 30 minutes, then drizzle over the honey and toss to coat evenly. Roast for another 10 minutes or until the vegetables are completely tender and lightly charred. Sprinkle over the sesame seeds and parsley and toss gently until evenly coated.

To Serve Tip the roasted root vegetables into a serving dish and place directly on the table so that people can help themselves.

Tip Try using any combination of root vegetables you fancy. However, it's probably worth remembering that beetroot will stain all other root vegetables, so it's probably best to roast them on their own.

Brussels Sprouts with Bacon

Serves 8-10

Choose Brussels sprouts that are as fresh as possible and look like tight round buttons. Take off the outer damaged leaves and using a small sharp knife, make a cross-wise incision at the stalk end of each one. This helps them to cook evenly and as quickly as the leaves.

Ingredients
6oz / 175g pine nuts (optional)
2lb / 900g Brussels sprouts, outer leaves removed and trimmed
2 tablespoons olive oil
1 large onion, finely chopped
10 rindless streaky bacon rashers, diced
2 garlic cloves, finely chopped
2oz / 50g butter
salt and freshly ground black pepper

Method Heat a frying pan and add the pine nuts, if using. Cook for a few minutes until evenly toasted, tossing occasionally to prevent them from burning. Tip into a bowl and set aside.

Place the Brussels sprouts in a pan of lightly salted water and bring to the boil, then reduce the heat and simmer for 4-5 minutes until tender.

Meanwhile, reheat the frying pan. Add the oil and then tip in the onion and bacon. Sauté for 2-3 minutes until the onion has softened and the bacon is beginning to crisp. Stir in the garlic and sauté for another minute or two until the bacon is crisp and lightly golden.

Drain the Brussels sprouts and return to the pan with the butter, tossing until melted. Add the bacon and onion mixture and the toasted pine nuts, if using. Stir until well combined and season to taste.

To Serve Tip the Brussels sprouts with bacon into a warmed serving dish and place directly on the table so that people can help themselves.

Tip If whole Brussels sprouts are not your thing, try grating them in a food processor and add to the bacon mixture that has been cooked in a large wok, then stir fry for another 3-4 minutes until tender.

Crispy Roast Potatoes with Thyme and Garlic

Serves 8-10

This recipe will give you really crunchy roast potatoes with fluffy middles. Choose a floury variety of potato and try to make sure that they are all similar in size. Cook them in the vegetable oil or better still use some fat that is leftover from a roast. It really does make the world of difference and as all fats freeze very well there's no excuse not to have some, especially for special occasions like Christmas Day. If you want to cook them and the roasted root vegetables with honey and parsley (page 111) for the same meal, just put these on the top shelf of the oven and the vegetables in the bottom, tossing the vegetables occasionally to prevent them from catching and burning.

Ingredients
3lb / 1.5kg potatoes, halved
about 3 ½fl oz / 100ml vegetable oil, or dripping, goose or duck fat (see intro.)
2 tablespoons fresh thyme leaves
6 garlic cloves, sliced
coarse sea salt

Method Place the potatoes in a pan of cold salted water and bring to the boil. Reduce the heat and simmer for 8-10 minutes until the outsides have just softened. Drain and return to the pan for a minute or two to dry out.

Meanwhile, preheat a roasting tin with a ½in / 1cm depth of oil, dripping, duck or goose fat for a few minutes until just smoking. Roughly prod the outside of the potatoes with a fork and toss them with thyme and garlic. Carefully tip them into the hot oil, basting the tops. Roast for about 45 minutes to 1 hour, turning occasionally, until crisp and golden.

To Serve Transfer the roast potatoes with a slotted spoon into a warmed serving bowl and season with the sea salt and place them directly on the table. Eat immediately - they don't hang around!

Tip To ensure really crispy roast potatoes drain off any excess fat about 20 minutes before the end of the cooking time. This will help them to go really crispy and golden brown around the edges.

Mulled Fruit Trifle

Serves 6

This is one dessert that I can clearly remember from my childhood - it probably even enticed me to be a chef. My Mum always made this for special occasions and I just loved helping, especially with the cleaning of the bowls . . . Frozen bags of fruits of the forest are available in most supermarkets, but you can experiment with any selection of frozen berries, or fruit for that matter. I just find them incredibly handy, when the fridge is bursting full with yummy things at Christmas.

Ingredients

1/4 pint / 150ml ruby red port
3oz / 75g caster sugar
1 teaspoon ground mixed spice
500g bag frozen fruits of the forest
7oz / 200g Madeira cake, broken into chunks
1/2 pint / 300ml cream

For the Custard

1/2 pint / 300ml milk
7fl oz / 200ml cream
5 egg yolks
4 tablespoons caster sugar
2 teaspoons cornflour
few drops vanilla essence
chocolate curls, to decorate

Method To make the custard, place the milk and cream in a heavy-based pan over a gentle heat and cook until it nearly reaches the boil - but don't allow to boil. Meanwhile, place the egg yolks, cornflour, sugar and vanilla essence in a large bowl and whisk together until pale and thickened.

Remove the milk and cream mixture from the heat and then slowly whisk it into the egg mixture until smooth. Pour back into the pan and place on a gentle heat. Cook, without allowing to boil, until the custard coats the back of a wooden spoon, stirring continuously. Remove from the heat and leave to cool. stirring occasionally to prevent a skin forming on top. Cover with cling film to prevent any skin forming.

Place the ruby red port in a large pan with the sugar and mixed spice and then bring to the boil. Reduce the heat and simmer for 5 minutes until syrupy, stirring occasionally. Stir in the frozen fruits of the forest and set aside until cooled, stirring occasionally. The fruits should defrost naturally in the hot syrup but still hold their shape.

Scatter the Madeira cake over the base of a 2 1/2 pint / 1.5 litre glass serving bowl. Spoon over the fruits of the forest mixture and cover with the cooled custard. Whip the cream in a bowl until you have achieved soft peaks and place spoonfuls on top of custard, then gently spread with a palette knife to cover the custard completely. Chill for 1 hour, or you can make this up to 24 hours in advance, but finish with the whipped cream just before serving.

To Serve Sprinkle the chocolate curls over the trifle and place straight on the table, then spoon into individual serving bowls.

Tip If disaster strikes and the custard becomes lumpy whilst you are still cooking it, don't panic - stop stirring and remove the pan from the heat. Strain the custard into a large jug, then cover with clingfilm to prevent a skin forming.

Gluten-Free Christmas Pudding

Serves 8

This gluten-free pud is so tasty non-coeliacs will love it too. It is kept moist with butter instead of suet and is lighted with fresh breadcrumbs. The quantities can also be halved to serve four and it could be steamed in any heatproof bowl or mould - old jelly moulds make lovely shapes. Try to make it in October or November so that it's perfect for Christmas (however, it is still wonderful if you have only had time to make it at the last minute!). Gluten-free products are available from well-stocked supermarkets and health food shops.

Ingredients
5oz / 150g fresh gluten-free bread
4oz / 100g butter, plus extra for greasing
2oz / 50g rice flour
1/2 teaspoon ground cinnamon
1 teaspoon mixed spice
1/2 teaspoon gluten-free baking powder
1 cooking apple, peeled, cored and grated (about 4oz / 100g)
1 carrot, grated (about 4oz / 100g)
14oz / 400g mixed dried fruit
4oz / 100g light muscovado sugar
2oz / 50g chopped mixed peel
2oz / 50g ground almonds
1 tablespoon black treacle
2 eggs, beaten
finely grated rind of 1/2 lemon and 1/2 orange
8 tablespoons dark rum
rum butter or pouring custard, to serve

Method Break the bread into pieces and place in a food processor or liquidiser and whiz to fine crumbs. Melt the butter in a small pan or in the microwave. Leave to cool a little. Sift the rice flour into a large bowl with the cinnamon, mixed spice and baking powder. Add the breadcrumbs, cooled melted butter, apple, carrot, mixed dried fruit, sugar, mixed peel and ground almonds. Mix thoroughly until well combined.

Heat the treacle in a small pan or in the microwave until just warmed through. Stir in the eggs, lemon and orange rind and two tablespoons of the rum, then mix into the dried fruit mixture until well combined. Spoon into a 2 1/2 pint / 1.25 litre pudding basin that has been greased and base-lined with non-stick parchment paper. Cover with a double circle of non-stick parchment paper, then place a double piece of buttered foil on top, pleated in the centre to allow room for expansion during cooking. Now secure with string, making a handle so that you can easily lift it out of the hot steamer.

Place the pudding on an upturned plate inside a large pan and pour in enough boiling water to come two-thirds up the sides of the basin. Steam for 4 hours until risen and firm to the touch, topping up with boiling water occasionally so as not to allow the pan to boil dry. Leave to cool completely, then cover the pudding basin with fresh non-stick parchment paper. Wrap in fresh foil and store in a cool dry place, feeding occasionally, if liked (see tip).

To Serve To reheat the pudding, steam as before for 2 hours. Remove the papers and turn out on to a warmed serving dish, then place on a heatproof mat on the table. Heat the remaining 6 tablespoons of rum in a small pan and pour over the pudding. Ignite with a match or taper, tipping the plate from time to time to burn off the alcohol. Cut into slices and arrange on warmed serving plates with some rum butter or custard, if liked.

Tip This pudding will benefit from 'feeding' during storage. Simply spear occasionally with a skewer and sprinkle over a couple of tablespoons of rum.

Christmas Drinks

Mulled Wine

Serves 4-6

You may need to alter the amount of sugar you use depending on how sweet your orange juice is. Just be careful that you do not allow the mixture to boil or you'll cook off the alcohol and ruin the appearance of the lemon and orange slices.

Ingredients
1 bottle red wine
1 pint / 600ml freshly squeezed orange juice
2-3oz / 50-75g caster sugar
2 cinnamon sticks, broken in half
12 whole cloves
6 whole star anise
1 lemon, halved and sliced
1 orange, halved and sliced

Method Place the wine in a pan with the orange juice, sugar, cinnamon, cloves and star anise, lemon and orange slices and heat gently for about 5 minutes to allow the flavours to combine, stirring occasionally, until the sugar has dissolved.

To Serve Ladle the mulled wine into heatproof glasses, making sure that some of the orange and lemon slices go into each one.

Tip Christmas is one of those celebrations when children are the heart of the event. Replace the wine with sparkling red grape juice so that everyone can enjoy this yummy drink equally.

Cranberry Fizz

Serves 6-8

Ingredients
1 bottle sparkling dry white wine, well chilled
8fl oz / 225ml cranberry juice, well chilled
fresh raspberries, to decorate

To Serve Fill tall long stemmed glasses two-thirds full with the wine. Top up with the cranberry juice. Decorate each one with a couple of raspberries.

Tip Place the glasses in the freezer for 1 hour before serving. This will give the glasses a wonderful frosted appearance and help keep the drinks well chilled.

Irish Coffee

Serves 2

A little indulgence is a wonderful thing and it doesn't come much better than this...a dark luxurious Irish coffee, topped with lightly whipped cream. What more could anyone ask for to finish off a sumptuous meal.

Ingredients
3fl oz / 85ml double cream, well chilled
2 tablespoons sugar
2 tablespoons Irish whiskey
½ pint / 300ml freshly brewed espresso coffee (piping hot)
pinch fresh grated nutmeg, to decorate (optional)

Method Heat a small heavy-based frying pan over a medium heat. Place the cream in a bowl and lightly whip, then chill until needed. Sprinkle the sugar over the base of the frying pan and allow to caramelise, without stirring. Pour in the whiskey and quickly flambé and then cook over a low heat until smooth, stirring occasionally. Remove from the heat and stir in the coffee until completely dissolved.

To Serve Pour into hefty, thick-stemmed glasses, then over the back of a spoon, carefully pour a layer of cream on top. Add a tiny grating of nutmeg, if liked.

Tip Add a couple of tablespoons of Baileys Irish cream or Kaluaha (coffee liqueur) for an extra kick.

Homemade Lemonade

Serves 4-6

Choose any variety of citrus fruit to make this drink, but I really do prefer the tangy sharpness of the lemons. Try using three limes, or replace half the quantity of water with freshly squeezed orange juice for a really rich flavour.

Ingredients
2 lemons, chopped (including pith and peel)
4-6 tablespoons caster sugar
1 pint / 600ml soda or sparkling water
8oz / 225g ice cubes
1 lime, sliced
fresh mint sprigs, to decorate

Method Blitz the lemons in a food processor or liquidiser with four tablespoons of the sugar and the water until well combined, then push through a sieve into a large jug. Taste. You may wish to add more sugar for a sweeter finish. Chill until needed. You may want to store this in a screw-topped bottle to keep the fizz if you plan to keep it for any length of time.

To Serve Fill sturdy tumbler-style glasses with ice cubes and top up with the lemonade, adding a couple of lime slices and mint sprigs to each one.

Tip Freeze tiny fresh mint sprigs in ice cubes, or experiment with tiny lemon and lime slices and/or raspberries.

Glossary

AL DENTE The texture of properly cooked pasta. Literally 'to the tooth' (Italian, it describes the slight resistance in the pasta when bitten.)
BASTE To spoon or brush a liquid (dripping from the pan, butter, fats or a marinade) over foods during roasting or grilling to keep moist.
BLANCH To parboil by immersing in rapidly boiling water for a few seconds or minutes.
BONED To remove fish bones from the fillet of round fish. Kitchen pliers or tweezers can be used.
BUTTER Unsalted butter can withstand higher temperatures than ordinary butter. Both can be used in recipes, but normally ordinary butter has a little oil added which prevents it from burning.
CARAMELISE To heat (particularly under a grill or with a blowtorch) so that the natural sugars in the food burn slightly and go brown. Sugar can also be sprinkled on food to create this effect, as in crème brûlée.
COULIS Fruit that is sweetened with sugar and thinned with water, then pureed to form a fruit sauce or garnish for desserts.
CREAM Irish cream has a similar fat content to double cream and is even richer in some cases.
CUSTARD A cooked or baked mixture, mainly of eggs and milk.
DICE To cut into very small cubes of similar size and shape.
DREDGE To coat food with flour or another powdered ingredient.
DRIZZLE To sprinkle drops of liquid erratically over food, usually for garnish.
EGGS Preferably free-range or organic, where possible. All recipes were tested using medium-sized eggs (size 3).
FOLD To blend two mixtures together gently, releasing as little air as possible. Cut gently through the mixture with a spatula or whisk, from the bottom to the top, rotating the bowl constantly, until thoroughly mixed.
GELATINE An unflavoured substance which gives body to mousses and desserts, and aids setting. Available in leaves or powdered form.
HULL To remove the tough part of fruit under the stalk, particularly strawberries.
LIGHT MUSCOVADO SUGAR This has a far superior caramelised flavour. Use instead of ordinary brown sugar that is just refined white sugar that has been coloured.
MARINADE An acidic-based liquid mixture combining various seasonings used to flavour and tenderise (particularly in meat cookery). Brush food with the mixture or marinate by immersing in it and leaving for at least 1-3 hours but preferably overnight.
MARINATE (also 'marinade'): To soak in a marinade.
PARSLEY There are two varieties, continental flat leaf and the more commonly used curly. Both can be used in recipes depending on preference.
POACH To cook very gently in any liquid kept just below boiling point.
PUREE To mash until perfectly smooth, either by hand, by putting through a sieve or by mixing in a food processor or liquidiser.
REDUCE To simmer a liquid until much of the moisture evaporates.
REFRESH To dip into cold water or run cold water over food that has been parboiled or 'blanched' in hot water. This stops food from cooking any further.
RIND Thin outer coloured layer of a citrus fruit's skin. Can be removed with a special zester, a vegetable peeler or box grater.
SAUTÉ To cook gently in a small amount of oil or butter on a low heat. Also used to brown food.
SEAL To brown very quickly on all sides to seal in juices and flavour and improve appearance and colour.
SEASONING A mixture of three parts salt to one part ground pepper.
SIMMER To keep a liquid or sauce at point just below boiling-point. When simmering, small bubbles will rise slowly to the surface, usually breaking before they reach it.
SWEAT To cook slowly in oil or butter.
SYRUP Sugar dissolved in liquid, usually water, over a medium heat. Syrup cooked until most of the liquid has evaporated becomes a caramel sauce.
WILT To cook until limp e.g. vegetables.